DR. KNOWLEDGE™ PRESENTS

Strange & Fascinating Facts about the Presidents

CHARLES REICHBLUM

Black Dog & Leventhal
Paperbacks

Published by

Black Dog & Leventhal Publishers, Inc.
151 West 19th Street
New York, NY 10011

Distributed by

Workman Publishing Company
708 Broadway
New York, NY 10003

Manufactured in the United States of America

Cover and interior design by Liz Driesbach
Illustrations by George Peters

ISBN: 1-57912-357-0

g f e d c b a

Library of Congress Cataloging-in-Publication Data
is on file at Black Dog & Leventhal Publishers, Inc.

Dedication

He works out of his house, but from that office in his home, he (and perhaps someday, she) holds what is arguably the biggest job in the world—the presidency of the United States.

There have been rich men, poor men, young men, old men, brilliant men, ordinary men, lucky men, and unlucky men who have been in the office for as long as twelve years or as short as thirty-two days.

This book explores the sometimes surprising, strange, and fascinating stories of these men, and is dedicated to the concept they swore to uphold—the concept of freedom and democracy.

On a more personal note, this book is dedicated to my family (Audrey, Bob, Diane, Rachel, Justin, Bill, Amalie, Noah, and Clarissa), and to the professional help from editor Kylie Foxx and literary agent Paula Litzky.

May you, dear reader, get as much enjoyment learning about the presidents as I did in researching and writing about them.

DR. KNOWLEDGE™ PRESENTS

Strange & Fascinating Facts about the Presidents

Three Times a Charm

At some point or another everyone complains that they have bad luck. But can you imagine if you were a bad luck *charm*? What if you alone had been on the scene of the assassinations of *three* different presidents?

This unfortunate fate befell Abraham Lincoln's son Robert. Robert was with his father the night Abraham was shot in 1865—and that was only the beginning of the unbelievable streak.

Sixteen years later, in 1881, Robert was secretary of war in President Garfield's cabinet. Garfield was leaving on a trip from a railroad station in Washington. Robert accompanied Garfield to the station, where Garfield was promptly shot with Robert standing just feet away.

Twenty years after that, in 1901, Robert was serving as head of the U.S. Chamber of Commerce and was invited by President McKinley to join him at a business exposition in Buffalo, New York. As Robert walked into the exhibition hall, he saw McKinley greeting people in a receiving line. Just then, McKinley was shot.

Not surprisingly, after McKinley's assassination Robert vowed that he would never again go near a president of the United States. He lived another twenty-five years and kept his vow. (Though it's unlikely any president would have invited him anyhow.)

And That's Not All!

Eerie coincidences seemed to be a trademark of Robert Lincoln's life. As a young boy he fell off a railroad platform just as a train was approaching. A man standing nearby saw what happened and quickly reached down to pull Robert off the tracks—probably saving Robert's life.

The boy's rescuer was a famous Shakespearean actor by the name of Edwin Thomas Booth. Edwin is in the Hall of Fame for Great Americans for his prestigious acting career, but it's Edwin's brother who is better remembered today. Edwin's brother was John Wilkes Booth—the man who later assassinated Robert's father, Abraham Lincoln.

A ROSE BY ANY OTHER NAME
Had John Adams had his way, instead of being called Mr. President, presidents would have been called "His Highness." He considered "president" too common a term, since it could apply to heads of all sorts of organizations.

FAST FACT

If Only He'd Paid Closer Attention . . .

When Al Gore was a student at Harvard in the late 1960s, he titled his senior thesis "The Impact of Television on the Presidency." That thesis helped him graduate with honors—but no one knew then that some thirty years later, when he would run for president himself in 2000, the impact of TV might cost him the presidency.

Many political observers felt Gore lost a good chunk of votes when he debated George W. Bush on television. The reason? His uptight, "wooden" demeanor and his seemingly condescending habit of sighing whenever Bush spoke. Not a good strategy, Al.

While Gore won the popular vote, he lost the electoral vote to Bush. Had Gore done better on TV and picked up just Florida or one or two other states, he would have won.

Perhaps Gore should have taken lessons from his roommate at Harvard. His roommate, the future actor Tommy Lee Jones, certainly could have taught Gore a thing or two about performing for the camera.

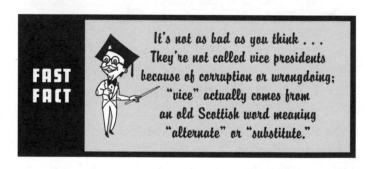

FAST FACT

It's not as bad as you think . . . They're not called vice presidents because of corruption or wrongdoing; "vice" actually comes from an old Scottish word meaning "alternate" or "substitute."

They're Playing Our Song . . . NOT!

During his presidency Gerald Ford honored Queen Elizabeth of England with a gala state dinner at the White House. As any good host would, President Ford asked the queen for a dance. He led Her

Majesty to the dance floor just as the U.S. Marine band began playing the next song on their music stands. Sounds lovely, right? Unfortunately, it was one of the most embarrassing moments in White House history. No, the president didn't trip the queen—instead, of all the songs in the world, he'd inadvertently asked her to dance to "The Lady Is a Tramp."

Luckily, the queen did not hold this musical mishap against President Ford or the United States.

Silent, but Snide

Have you ever heard of a politician who didn't love to talk? Calvin Coolidge, the thirtieth president, was not your run-of-the-mill politico. Coolidge was dubbed "Silent Cal" for good reason: He was an austere New Englander who wasn't fond of making speeches or even small talk.

One night, Silent Cal piqued the curiosity of a young woman seated next to him at a White House dinner party. "Mr. President," she said, "I made a bet with a friend that I could get you to say more than three words to me tonight." Coolidge turned to her and replied coolly, "You lose."

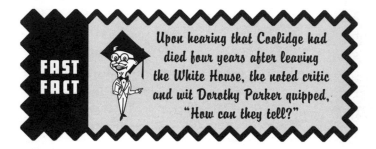

FAST FACT

Upon hearing that Coolidge had died four years after leaving the White House, the noted critic and wit Dorothy Parker quipped, "How can they tell?"

Popular, and on a Roll

Did you know that since 1860 the Democrats have *never* put more than two consecutive presidents into the White House? The only times the Democrats have had two presidents in a row were when Franklin Roosevelt and Harry Truman served between 1933 and 1953, and when John Kennedy and Lyndon Johnson were in office from 1961 to 1969.

The Republicans have had better luck than their rivals. They hold the record for most consecutive presidents, with four in a row—Ulysses Grant, Rutherford Hayes, James Garfield, and Chester Arthur—from 1869 to 1885.

The GOP also holds the number two position: Twice they've had three consecutive presidents—

William McKinley, Theodore Roosevelt, and William Howard Taft (1897–1913); and Warren Harding, Calvin Coolidge, and Herbert Hoover (1921–1933).

Sixteen of the twenty-five men elected president between 1860 and 2000 were Republicans.

FAST FACT

Prolific, but Not Creative

John Tyler fathered more children than any other president—eight by his first wife, seven by his second—a grand total of a whopping fifteen. Tyler may have been prolific, but he certainly didn't win any awards for creativity: When it came to naming all of these children, he ran out of ideas.

Tyler didn't let the fact that he'd already named two of his sons Robert and John stop him from using the exact same names for two later-born sons! Can you imagine the confusion this must have caused at the holidays?

FAST FACT

There have been no only-child presidents. Every single president has had at least one brother or sister.

Don't Count Your Chickens . . .

Nothing proved that old cliché more than the race between Harry Truman and Thomas Dewey in 1948. Virtually every poll predicted an overwhelming victory for Dewey. *Life* magazine went so far as to publish a picture of Dewey before the election with the title "The Next President," and the *Chicago Tribune*, so sure of Dewey's victory on election night, printed and distributed an early edition with the headline "Dewey Defeats Truman."

To the nation's surprise, however, Truman got over two million more votes than Dewey and won the Electoral College vote by 303 to 189. It wasn't even close—and Truman had won the biggest upset in U.S. presidential history.

How did it happen? Truman ran a down-to-earth, aggressive campaign, "giving 'em hell." He appealed to America's love of the underdog: One woman was quoted as saying she voted for Truman because she felt sorry for him. As for Dewey, he was perhaps lulled into overconfidence in the last weeks before the election. Whatever the cause, Truman delighted for years in holding up a copy of that infamous *Chicago Tribune* headline.

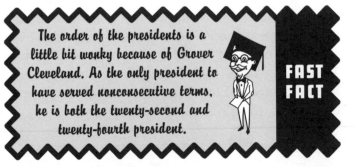

The order of the presidents is a little bit wonky because of Grover Cleveland. As the only president to have served nonconsecutive terms, he is both the twenty-second and twenty-fourth president.

FAST FACT

Bright, but Broke

Is there anything Thomas Jefferson couldn't do? He was good at so many things—he was a brilliant political thinker, author of the Declaration of Independence, diplomat, architect, inventor, scientific farmer, musician, founder of the prestigious University of Virginia, creator of the decimal system of coinage for the U.S., effective president, and one of the great figures in American history—but sadly, he was not good at managing money. Jefferson enjoyed fine living and often outspent his income to support his lavish lifestyle.

Jefferson had done so much for this country that many tried to help. Congress overpaid Jefferson for his book collection, and members of the public, who often had much less than Jefferson, made contributions to his cause. But all this help was too little, too late; when he died in 1826, he had racked up over $100,000 of debt. In today's terms, that'd be like $1.5 million! Jefferson's family, stuck with this debt, had no choice but to sell Jefferson's beloved home, Monticello, to help settle the debt.

FAST FACT

James Monroe was so broke when he left the White House that he had to move in with his daughter.

A Costly Lesson to Learn

It's hard not to wonder how history might have changed if John Parker, President Lincoln's one and only guard at Ford's Theatre, had stayed at his post. For some unknown reason, Parker left the doorway to the president's box for a brief time—just long enough for John Wilkes Booth to slip in and shoot the president.

Everyone wanted to know why Parker walked away. An inquiry was held, but somehow the records were lost, and no one today knows the answer. There were rumors that Parker stepped out to have a beer, but he was never charged and, in fact, continued in his job. He even served as a guard for Lincoln's successor, Andrew Johnson.

It was a costly lesson to learn. Today presidents *always* travel with more than one guard.

Risky Business

Would you take a job with a nearly twenty percent chance of death? Well, that's the rate for the presidency: Nearly one in every five presidents has died in office.

Abraham Lincoln was shot by John Wilkes Booth, a sympathizer for the South's cause in the Civil War, while watching "Our American Cousin" at Ford's Theatre in Washington, D.C., on Good Friday, April 14, 1865. James Garfield was shot by a disappointed office seeker, Charles Guiteau, at the Baltimore and Potomac railroad station in Washington, D.C., on July 2, 1881. William McKinley was shot by an anarchist, Leon Czolgosz, at a business exposition in Buffalo, New York, on September 6, 1901. And John Kennedy was shot in Dallas by Lee Harvey Oswald, whose motive is still not known, on November 22, 1963.

The remaining four, William Henry Harrison, Zachary Taylor, Warren Harding, and Franklin Roosevelt, all died of natural causes.

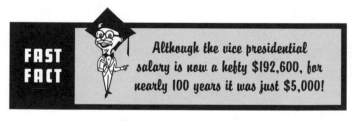

FAST FACT

Although the vice presidential salary is now a hefty $192,600, for nearly 100 years it was just $5,000!

And You Thought Thirty-Five Days Was a Long Time?

Imagine waiting four months after an election to find out the name of the next president. That's how long it took back in 1876 to figure out which candidate—Rutherford B. Hayes or Samuel Tilden—was the winner.

It wasn't a matter of slow vote counting, either. The delay was caused by a dispute over the electoral votes of four states—Florida, Louisiana, Oregon, and South Carolina. Voters in these states were not re-polled. Instead, the question of the next President was thrown into Congress, where it was hotly debated. Finally, a 15-man committee was chosen to select the winner. After a close 8–7 vote, Rutherford Hayes was named the victor 115 days after election day! And you thought waiting 35 days for the 2000 Bush-Gore decision was bad!

The Deal That Sealed It

The Democrats were not just disappointed that Samuel Tilden lost to Rutherford Hayes, they were furious. You see, the fifteen-man committee that selected the nineteenth president was comprised of eight Republicans and seven Democrats. It's no wonder the Republican Hayes won.

The Democrats were prepared to challenge the vote but instead proposed a deal. It was the aftermath of the Civil War, and the Democrats vowed they would accept the committee's decision if the new Republican administration withdrew all federal troops from the South. The Republicans weighed their options and decided to accept. The troops were withdrawn, the Southern states regained political control over their state and local governments, and Hayes moved into the White House.

Cool as a Cat

It took a lot to ruffle Harry Truman's feathers. Early on the afternoon of Nov. 1, 1950, two Puerto Rican nationalists tried to shoot their way into Blair House, where President Truman was staying while the White House was being renovated. One Secret Service man was killed and two others were wounded before the guards were able to kill one would-be assassin and capture the other.

President Truman, who had been upstairs at the time, was unhurt and apparently unshaken. Not only did he go out an hour later for a dedication cere-mony at Arlington National Cemetery, he kept the rest of his appointments that day and even took his usual walk the next morning.

Truman's comment on the incident? He brushed it off, saying, "A president has to expect these things."

Give 'em hell, Harry!

Age Discrimination?

Thomas Jefferson, George Washington, James Madison, John Adams, and Benjamin Franklin—men whose philosophy created the Declaration of Independence, the Constitution, and the Bill of Rights—are often cited among the leaders of the American Revolution and the Founding Fathers of the United States.

And all of them became presidents, except for one: Benjamin Franklin. It wasn't because Franklin wasn't bright or accomplished—he was called "the greatest man in the country" by Jefferson and was often sought for advice by the others. So what stopped him from officially leading the nascent country? It was his age. Franklin was eighty-three years old when the younger Washington, then fifty-seven, was selected as president. Franklin died a year later.

The Mystery of the "Illegal" President

Though Chester Arthur, the twenty-first president, always claimed he was born in Fairfield, Vermont, some suspect that he was actually born in Canada. This might not seem like a big deal, except there's a little rule in the Constitution that no person born outside the United States may become president.

So, why the mystery?

The questions about Arthur's birthplace arise because his father was an itinerant Baptist preacher who, like many rural ministers then, kept moving from one place to another. The family is known to have lived in many villages in Vermont, upstate New York, and Canada.

What historians just don't know is exactly where Arthur was born. After he became president, there were rumors that his parents were in Canada at the time of his birth. Arthur always denied it and stuck by his Vermont story. No definite proof, one way or the other, has ever been established. We'll probably never know for sure if Arthur was an "illegal" president or not.

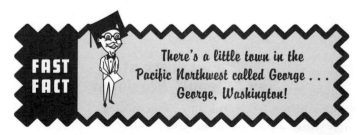

FAST FACT

There's a little town in the Pacific Northwest called George . . . George, Washington!

Paying Homage

John Kennedy hosted a White House dinner one evening for a group of Nobel Prize winners and others who had achieved intellectual success.

Kennedy toasted the group by saying that there was more brainpower in the dining room that night than at any other time in White House history—with the possible exception of when Thomas Jefferson dined alone. Now *that's* a compliment.

If Only
He'd Had More Time

President James Garfield was one talented fellow. Not only was he ambidextrous, a feat in and of itself, but he amazed White House guests by writing in Latin with one hand and Greek with the other—at the same time.

This was just one example of his intellectual prowess. Garfield had attended both Hiram and Williams Colleges, and then taught not only Latin and Greek but also mathematics, history, philosophy, and English literature—and wrote poetry.

He became one of the youngest college presidents of all time when he was appointed head of Hiram at age twenty-six, and that was only the beginning of his incredibly versatile career. Garfield went on to study law, was admitted to the bar, served as a general in the Civil War, and was elected to the U.S. House of Representatives and the U.S. Senate before becoming president of the United States.

Sadly, this multitalented president was shot just three months into his term and died from the wound just two short months later. Imagine what he could have done if he'd only had more time!

Right Family, Wrong Brother

Dwight Eisenhower and his brother Edgar were in the same high school class in Abilene, Kansas, even though they were about a year apart in age. The brothers made such an impression on their classmates that when they graduated in the class of 1909, their high school yearbook predicted that Dwight would grow up to become a history professor and

Edgar would someday be president of the United States. Hope there weren't too many bets riding on that!

The president's salary has risen by 1600 percent—from $25,000 to $400,000—in just over 200 years.

FAST FACT

not Sleepless in Seattle— or Anywhere Else

Calvin Coolidge, U.S. vice president in 1923, was home sleeping in Vermont when word came late at night that President Harding had died.

Coolidge's father, a justice of the peace, woke him up and gave him the oath of office. Coolidge then performed his first act as president of the United States. No, he didn't issue a big statement or snap a photo— instead, he went right back to bed. You might find this surprising, but it didn't come as such a shock: Coolidge had a reputation for enjoying his z's and was reported to have slept as much as eleven hours a day.

FDR Almost Stopped Before He Started

America's longest-serving president, Franklin D. Roosevelt, who led the nation for twelve years through the Great Depression and World War II, came within inches of having his first term snuffed out less than a month before he took office.

Roosevelt was to be inaugurated for the first of his four terms on March 4, 1933. But on Feb. 15, 1933, he was in Miami for a speech when an unemployed bricklayer, Giuseppe Zangara, tried to assassinate him. Zangara fired a shot at Roosevelt, but it hit and killed the mayor of Chicago, Anton Cermak, who was standing next to FDR. Zangara fired four more shots and wounded five other people.

Roosevelt was unharmed but came incredibly close to never being president. How different the history of the U.S. and the world might have been had Zangara's shots hit their intended target.

What drove Zangara to this deadly act? He later said he had "visions of killing a great ruler." And what became of Zangara? In near-record swiftness in punishing a capital crime, he was electrocuted just thirty-three days later, on March 20, 1933, at the Florida State Prison in Raiford, Florida.

Lucky Number 4

Almost all the major events in Calvin Coolidge's life happened on the fourth of a month.

He was born on July 4, 1872; got married on October 4, 1905; became U.S. vice president on March 4, 1921; and was elected president on November 4, 1924. (Incidentally, Coolidge was the only president born on the 4th of July.)

He managed to keep his lucky streak intact by making death wait until the fifth—the fifth of January, 1933.

> Though the Speaker of the House of Representatives is high on the list in presidential succession, James Polk was the only one to successfully claim the position.
>
> **FAST FACT**

Pigskin Presidents

Can you guess which four presidents graced the college football field? Gerald Ford had the best gridiron career of the four. He played center for University of Michigan teams that won the national championship in 1932 and 1933. In 1934, his senior year, he was voted the Most Valuable Player for Michigan. Ford was then invited to try out with several NFL teams, but turned them down because he wanted to continue his education and go to law school.

Dwight Eisenhower had a brief college football career as a halfback at the U.S. Military Academy at West Point in 1911, and two other presidents played college football at small schools: Richard Nixon was a lineman at Whittier College in Whittier, California, from 1931–1933; and Ronald Reagan was a halfback for Eureka College in Eureka, Illinois, from 1930–1931.

Team Spirit

It all came down to one big game. Army was playing Carlisle in 1911. That doesn't sound like a big deal, but at that time Carlisle was a national power—and their star was one of the greatest players of all time, a future Hall of Famer named Jim Thorpe. The national press covered the Army-Carlisle game, in part because of Thorpe's presence.

Early in the game, Thorpe got the ball and started one of his storied runs. Dwight Eisenhower, a West Point cadet, tried to tackle Thorpe. Not only didn't Ike make the tackle, but he broke his leg trying to stop and pin down the elusive Thorpe.

Although he was only a freshman at the time, Eisenhower never played college football again.

On, and Off, the Field

Although Ronald Reagan played college football at little Eureka College, his most memorable football connection happened off the field—when he was a young actor in Hollywood.

In the movie *Knute Rockne—All American*, Reagan played Notre Dame's great Hall of Fame star George Gipp. Gipp had become ill after the last game of his senior season, and lying on his deathbed, gave Coach Knute Rockne the basis for football's most famous pep talk.

Reagan reenacted the scene in the film, telling Rockne, "I've got to go now, Rock. It's all right. But sometime, Rock, when the team's up against it; when things are wrong and the breaks are beating the boys, tell them to go in there with all they've got—and win one for the Gipper."

In real life, the speech became famous when Rockne used it at halftime of the Notre Dame– Army game in 1928, rallying Notre Dame to victory. Reagan never forgot that speech, and even as president, "winning one for the Gipper" was one of his favorite sayings.

All in the Family

It sounds like daytime TV, but it's real. The year 1886 was a big one for Frances Folsom: She turned twenty-one, married her surrogate father, and became the youngest-ever first lady. How, you ask? Frances's real father died when she was ten, leaving her the legal ward of her late father's law partner, Grover Cleveland.

Eleven years later, in 1886, Grover Cleveland was president of the United States. Cleveland, then forty-nine years old and a lifelong bachelor up to that time, took Ms. Folsom as his bride in the White House.

Aside from making Frances the youngest-ever first lady, Grover Cleveland added another bit of history to that wedding. He became the only president to be married at the White House.

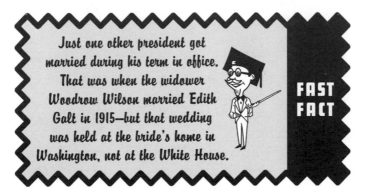

Just one other president got married during his term in office. That was when the widower Woodrow Wilson married Edith Galt in 1915—but that wedding was held at the bride's home in Washington, not at the White House.

FAST FACT

Now That's Dedication

President Benjamin Harrison was scared to death of the newly invented electric lights that were installed in the White House for the first time in 1891. He feared if he touched a light switch on the wall, he'd get a shock.

So Harrison used old-style gaslights on his desk and insisted an aide turn the electric lights on and off for him. That aide must have been dedicated, or fearless!

America's Leading Family?

Can you guess which one family has held ten high governmental offices within just three generations? If you guessed Bush, you'd be right!

Prescott Bush was a U.S. senator from Connecticut.

His son, George H. W. Bush, was a U.S. congressman from Texas, ambassador to the U.N. and to China, head of the CIA, and vice president and president of the United States.

One of George H. W.'s sons, Jeb, became governor of Florida.

His other son, George W., was governor of Texas, and became president of the United States. Only time will tell what the Bushes will do next!

The Adams Family

One family has got the Bushes beat—the Adamses. John Adams was a delegate to the Continental Congress; ambassador to France, the Netherlands, and England; and vice president and president of the United States.

His son, John Quincy, was ambassador to the Netherlands, Russia, and England; U.S. secretary of state; a member of the U.S. Senate and House; and U.S. president.

John's grandson, Charles, was an ambassador to England, a member of the U.S. House—and came close to giving America its first father-son-grandson presidential combination. There was talk about running Charles for president in several elections, but he never got a nomination.

Still, the Adams family held a total of fifteen high government offices. Think the Bushes will catch up?

Doctor President? Though presidents often have stellar résumés, only one president came to the White House with a Ph.D.—Woodrow Wilson.

FAST FACT

No Degree Necessary

It may sound strange, but many of the men who've held the highest office in the land did not have a higher education. Almost one-fifth of all U.S. presidents never went to college—and that includes two of the greatest, George Washington and Abraham Lincoln.

In all, nine presidents never attended college. Besides Washington and Lincoln, the others were Andrew Jackson, Martin Van Buren, Zachary Taylor, Millard Fillmore, Andrew Johnson, Grover Cleveland, and Harry Truman.

Going to college wasn't always as common as it seems today. In the 1700s and 1800s many boys in the United States spent their childhoods working, and went to grade or high school only sporadically. That was the case with Washington, Jackson, Van Buren, Taylor, Lincoln, Fillmore, and Cleveland. They never considered college. Johnson didn't go to school at all as a child and never learned to read or write until his girlfriend taught him when he was seventeen years old.

Truman was the last president to date without a college education. He attended elementary and high school, but after graduating from high school, he went to work—entering the "college of hard knocks" with a series of jobs and a failed haberdashery business. This eventually led up to his entry into politics, and, finally, the highest office in the land.

Slave-Owning Presidents

It's hard to believe, but the man who wrote the Declaration of Independence was a slave owner.

That was future president Thomas Jefferson, who penned these immortal lines: "All men are created equal . . . endowed by their Creator with certain unalienable rights, that among these are life, liberty and the pursuit of happiness."

Yet Jefferson had more than 100 slaves at his Monticello estate. And he wasn't alone. Among the early presidents who owned slaves were George Washington, James Madison, James Monroe, Andrew Jackson, John Tyler, James Polk, Zachary Taylor, and Andrew Johnson. Perhaps even more surprising, Ulysses Grant, the commander of the Northern forces in the Civil War, had owned slaves on his Missouri farm before the war.

Reflecting on a conversation with an advocate for the preservation of slavery, Abraham Lincoln said, "I felt a strong impulse to see it tried on him personally."

FAST FACT

Family Foes

In 1835 there was a colonel in the U.S. Army who took less than a liking to one of his lieutenants, a man from

Mississippi. To make matters worse, this lieutenant, who ostensibly could have pursued any other woman, wanted to marry the colonel's daughter.

Of course the colonel opposed the marriage, but his daughter and the lieutenant defied his wishes and eloped. The colonel, as you might imagine, was not pleased.

But the story didn't end there. . . . Fast-forward a few years. In 1849, the colonel, who in the meantime had become a general, was elected president of the United States. His name: Zachary Taylor. And Taylor's son-in-law, the lieutenant, eventually became a U.S. senator. But he achieved even more fame in 1861, when he was selected as the president of the Confederacy during the Civil War. His name: Jefferson Davis.

The Trip That Started It All

President Teddy Roosevelt had no idea when he traveled from the White House in 1902 to Louisiana for a bear-hunting trip that he would inspire a multimillion-dollar industry.

The president's hosts wanted to make sure he had a bear to shoot at (it was a bear-hunting trip, after all). But the only bear they found for him was a cub—and the president refused to shoot the furry little guy. The next day Roosevelt found himself something of a hero. Stories splashed the newspapers about how Teddy had compassionately spared the little cub's life.

Shortly thereafter, Morris and Rose Mitchom, owners of a candy store in Brooklyn, New York, began to make and sell new stuffed toy animals resembling small bears.

They named them after the president who wouldn't shoot—Teddy Roosevelt—and since then, millions of teddy bears have been sold worldwide.

Teddy Roosevelt got no royalties for the use of his name, but apparently was happy that a favorite children's toy was named after him.

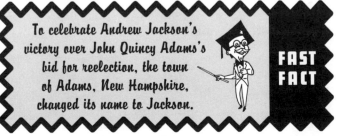

To celebrate Andrew Jackson's victory over John Quincy Adams's bid for reelection, the town of Adams, New Hampshire, changed its name to Jackson.

FAST FACT

Getting Our Say

Did you know that the general public did not vote George Washington into office? And he wasn't the only president elected that way—popular voting for presidents was virtually nonexistent for the first thirty-nine years of presidential elections.

In those days, state legislatures usually picked members of the Electoral College who then voted to choose a president. Average citizens did not have the chance to vote in a presidential election.

Besides Washington, five other presidents were not elected by the public. They were John Adams, Thomas Jefferson, James Madison, James Monroe, and John Quincy Adams.

The public finally got their say when Andrew Jackson became president. For it was in 1828 when the popular vote—and not the state legislatures—largely determined the electors in the Electoral College, who then voted for the candidate receiving the most popular votes in their state.

Almost Unanimous

George Washington was so popular, and was such an obvious choice to lead the nation, that he received every vote for president in the Electoral College and was elected unanimously for both his terms.

One other president, James Monroe, almost matched that.

When James Monroe ran for his second term in 1820, the nation was enjoying what was called "the era of good feeling." Times were generally good for the country and there was no real opposition to Monroe. All the electors in the Electoral College voted for Monroe with one exception. William Plummer of New Hampshire cast his vote for John Quincy Adams—not because he was opposed to Monroe, but because he felt no one other than Washington should be honored with a unanimous election.

Since then no other president has faced as little opposition in the nation as Monroe did. And thanks to Plummer, Washington's historic record was preserved.

Presidential Mug Shots

Sometimes presidents seem to be above the law. But did you know that presidents can be arrested, and that two already have been?!

When Franklin Pierce was president in 1853, he was driving to the White House by horse and carriage when he ran down an elderly woman. The woman was injured, though not seriously, and Pierce was arrested by a constable. Fortunately for Pierce, neither the victim nor the police decided to press charges, so the case was dropped.

President Ulysses Grant was also arrested in Washington for speeding in his carriage. When the arresting police officer realized who Grant was, he offered to withhold a ticket, but Grant told him to do his duty. Grant put up twenty dollars as collateral, which he forfeited when he failed to appear for the hearing. Later Grant wrote the officer's superior commending him for what he had done.

Sore Losers

When John Adams lost his reelection bid to Thomas Jefferson, he was so bitter that he refused to attend Jefferson's inauguration. On the morning of inauguration day, on March 4, 1801, hours before the ceremonies were to start, Adams left Washington and began his journey home to Massachusetts.

Oddly enough, his son, John Quincy, did the same thing. When John Quincy left his presidency, on

March 4, 1829, he didn't show up at the inauguration of his successor, Andrew Jackson.

Only two other presidents who were living at the time failed to attend the swearing in of their successor. The first was Andrew Johnson, who disliked Ulysses Grant so much he refused to attend his inauguration in 1869. The second was Richard Nixon. After Nixon announced his resignation on the evening of August 8, 1974, he left for his home in California the next morning and was gone by the time Gerald Ford took the oath of office at noon.

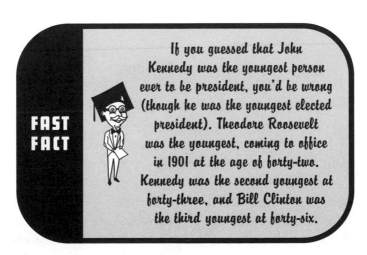

FAST FACT

If you guessed that John Kennedy was the youngest person ever to be president, you'd be wrong (though he was the youngest elected president). Theodore Roosevelt was the youngest, coming to office in 1901 at the age of forty-two. Kennedy was the second youngest at forty-three, and Bill Clinton was the third youngest at forty-six.

The Youngest Almost President

The closest the U.S. has come to having a president younger than forty years old was during the administration of James Buchanan.

Buchanan's vice president, John Breckinridge, was only thirty-six when he was inaugurated as the youngest VP in history.

President Buchanan served out his term, but had anything happened during the first three years of his term, Breckinridge would have assumed the presidency while still just in his thirties.

Landslide Lyndon

Lyndon Johnson's political career got off to a peculiar start. Johnson ran for the U.S. Senate from Texas in 1948. Popular former governor Coke Stevenson beat Johnson in the primary by a margin of 70,000 votes, but failed to get a majority of the total votes cast in a ten-person field, so a runoff election was mandated. In the runoff, Stevenson was originally thought to have won, but a recount was ordered in one county where 202 suspicious ballots suddenly turned up, all for Johnson.

Those suspicious ballots gave Johnson an eighty-seven-vote win. Stevenson charged fraud, but Johnson was officially declared the winner and went to the Senate with the sarcastic nickname "Landslide Lyndon."

In the Senate, Johnson made his mark, rising to majority leader. From there, he went on to the vice presidency, and presidency. Way to go, Landslide!

At Home for the Homicide

Presidents and vice presidents don't typically travel together, but strangely enough VP Lyndon Johnson was on the scene in Dallas when President John Kennedy was assassinated on November 22, 1963.

Johnson was riding just two cars behind Kennedy when fatal shots rang out at their motorcade. Immediately, a Secret Service man jumped on Johnson, threw him to the floor of his automobile, and lay on top of him.

The cars with Kennedy and Johnson then sped to Parkland Hospital, where Kennedy was pronounced dead. Just one hour and thirty nine minutes later, at 2:39 P.M., Johnson was sworn in as the new president on Air Force One, parked at Love Field in Dallas, with Mrs. Kennedy standing beside him.

Johnson had become the first vice president to witness his predecessor's assassination. And why did Johnson just happen to be there? Not for any strategic reason—he was mainly in Dallas just to visit his home state.

The Rumor Mill

In Victorian times when James Buchanan was president, from 1857 to 1861, not many people spoke openly about homosexuality, but political opponents and others began a whispering campaign that Buchanan was homosexual. Why, you wonder?

Buchanan was the only president who never married, although he was engaged to Ann Coleman of Lancaster, Pennsylvania, when he was twenty-eight years old. She died, however, before their proposed wedding, and the gossip of the day was that she had committed suicide after he broke off the engagement.

By the time he ran for president at age sixty-five, rumors had increased about Buchanan, fueled by the fact that he had lived for many years with a close male friend, a bachelor senator from Alabama, William R. King.

The Victorians may have been more open-minded than we give them credit for, since Buchanan had no trouble being elected president. He scored a convincing victory over his main opponent, John Fremont. Buchanan received about 500,000 more popular votes than Fremont and almost one million more votes than the third-party candidate, former president Millard Fillmore.

The Remote Vice President

James Buchanan's friend William R. King ended his twenty-nine-year career as a U.S. senator when he was elected vice president under Franklin Pierce in 1852—and similar to the talk about President Buchanan's sexual orientation, there were those who said King was homosexual.

King lasted only six weeks as VP. Before his inauguration, King had gone to Cuba to recuperate from an illness. For inauguration day, he was too ill to come to Washington but by a special act of Congress, he was permitted to take his oath of office in Havana, Cuba.

King thus became the first and only president or vice president to take the oath in a foreign country. He died forty-five days after inauguration day and never did make it to Washington while he was vice president.

In those days there was no Constitutional provision for replacing a vice president, so President Pierce went through virtually his entire term without a VP. If something had happened to Pierce, the Speaker of the House of Representatives would have become president.

Something in the Genes?

Barbara Bush is not only the mother of the forty-third U.S. president, George W. Bush, and the wife of the forty-first president, George H. W. Bush, but she's also related to the fourteenth president.

Barbara's maiden name was Pierce. Her father, Marvin Pierce, was a descendant of Franklin Pierce, who was president from 1853 to 1857.

That was Marvin's only connection to politics. He was in the magazine business and became chief executive of *McCall's* magazine. He and his wife, Pauline, sent their daughter Barbara to Ashley Hall, a private girls' boarding school in South Carolina. While home from school at Christmastime in Rye,

New York, Barbara was invited to a dance with the boys from Phillips Academy of Andover, Massachusetts. It was at that party that sixteen-year-old Barbara met a Phillips boy that she liked. The two began dating and got married four years later, in 1945. And a year after that, George and Barbara Bush welcomed their first child, George W. Bush, into the world.

First Lady Senator

Hillary Clinton made history in 2000 when she ran for the U.S. Senate seat from New York. This marked the first time the wife of an incumbent president entered an election for a high political office and won.

In fact, it was the first time ever that any president's wife ran for an elective office.

The funny thing is that Mrs. Clinton won a seat from New York, even though she wasn't from there. She was born and grew up in Illinois and lived for many years in Arkansas. But Clinton was able to run for another state due to the following quirk in the Constitution: Someone may be elected to the Senate as long as he or she is a resident of the state they will represent *when* elected. So all Hillary had to do to represent New York was to establish a residence there by election day. She did just that, and in a historic moment, changed titles from First Lady Clinton to Senator Clinton.

That's "Mister Washington" to You

After the Revolutionary War, George Washington was held in such high esteem, and had such an air of authority even before he became president, that no one dared call him by his first name.

But one story has it that after a long, hard day at the Constitutional Convention, Alexander Hamilton bet Pennsylvania delegate Gouverneur Morris that Morris didn't have the guts to walk up to Washington, slap him on the back, and say, "Hi, George." As far as bets go, this may not seem like a big one, but it was. Not only was Washington an intimidating character, but at that time such informal greetings were unheard of. Still Morris, though perhaps daunted, took the bet.

Morris bravely strode over to Washington with Hamilton and others looking on, and went ahead with the audacious hello. Washington did not respond. Morris said later that the look Washington gave him made him wish he had never done it.

First Lady of Espionage

What if the first lady were a spy? That was a question on the minds of many when First Lady Mary Todd Lincoln, wife of Abraham Lincoln, was accused of being one during the Civil War.

On what basis? Well, Mrs. Lincoln was a Southerner, born in Kentucky. Her brother, George, was a surgeon in the Confederate army and several of her half brothers and brothers-in-law were Confederate soldiers.

Because of this, some congressmen and others suspected she was passing secrets to Southern forces.

The suspicions were so rampant that President Lincoln went before Congress and made this statement: "I, of my own knowledge, know that it is untrue that any member of my family holds treasonable relations with the enemy."

Even though no spy charges were ever filed against Mrs. Lincoln, things did not get much easier for her. After the Civil War and the assassination of her husband, Mrs. Lincoln was forced before a Court of

Inquest because she'd suffered years of mental illness. The court ordered her "committed to a state hospital for the insane."

FAST FACT

As an actor, Ronald Reagan portrayed practically everything except a governor and a president—the two real jobs he held post-Hollywood.

Sticking Close to the Role

Ronald Reagan's first wife, movie star Jane Wyman, won the Academy Award for Best Actress without ever saying a word.

She won the Oscar for her role in the 1948 film *Johnny Belinda* in which she played a deaf mute. Upon winning the award, Wyman gave one of the shortest acceptance speeches in Academy history. She said, "I won this award by keeping my mouth shut, and I'm going to do the same thing again."

Wyman, whose real name was Sarah Jane Fulks, met Reagan when they starred together in a 1938 movie, *Brother Rat*. They married in 1940, but divorced shortly after Wyman won her Oscar.

The Unexpected President

Lots of people were surprised that James Polk became president—including him!

When the Democrats met to choose their nominee at the 1844 convention, Polk wasn't a candidate. His name wasn't even mentioned on the first seven ballots. But the convention was deadlocked and delegates needed a compromise nominee, so they turned to Polk. Polk was the underdog to the more famous Henry Clay in that fall's election. Clay seized on Polk's low profile and campaigned with the slogan "Who is James Polk?" His campaign worked—but not for him! Polk won in one of the biggest upsets in presidential history.

The only comparable upset was Harry Truman's win over Thomas Dewey in 1948, but Truman was expected to at least run in that race, and was already president when he ran, whereas Polk was an unlikely candidate to begin with. So Polk goes down with the dubious honor of being one of the most unexpected men ever to be elected president of the United States.

So, Who Was James Polk?

Polk was a mere speck on the public radar at the time of his election. He was a Tennessee lawyer who had been elected to the U.S. House of Representatives. There, he was a loyal Democratic party man, and rose to the position of Speaker of the House— the only Speaker in history who would become a U.S. president.

But life in Washington was not for him. After serving in Congress, he returned home to run for governor of Tennessee in 1839. He won a two-year term then, but lost reelection tries in 1841 and 1843, and seemed finished politically.

Washington wasn't done with him, though. The delegates at the 1844 Democratic presidential convention just couldn't agree on a candidate. Ballot after ballot was taken with no one getting the necessary votes. Finally, one delegate, George Bancroft of Massachusetts, brought up Polk's name. The exhausted convention finally accomplished two things: They chose Polk—almost out of desperation—and created a new political phrase. Polk became known as a "dark horse," an unexpectedly nominated candidate. In the ensuing race for president, this dark horse came in first.

Go, Gerry, Go!

When Geraldine Ferraro was selected by the Democrats to be their vice presidential candidate in 1984, she became the first woman to run on a major-party ticket for president or vice president. Ferraro was a U.S. congresswoman from New York when she was chosen to be the running mate with Walter Mondale.

Though she had lively debates with her Republican counterpart, George H. W. Bush, during the campaign, she and Mondale were soundly beaten in the election by Ronald Reagan and Bush. It wasn't meant to be for Geraldine, but perhaps one day soon we'll have our first Ms. President . . .

His Name Was Mudd

After he shot Abraham Lincoln at Ford's Theatre, John Wilkes Booth jumped out of the box where Lincoln had been sitting, and tripped—ironically—on an American flag draped in front of the box. As he fell, Booth broke his leg, but was still able to make his getaway.

While a fugitive-at-large, Booth found a doctor, Samuel Mudd, to set his leg. Though Mudd always claimed he didn't recognize Booth, he was sentenced to life in prison as an accessory to the crime after Booth was captured and shot a short time later.

Some felt Dr. Mudd's sentence was unjust, and after four years in prison, he was pardoned by President Andrew Johnson. A factor in his pardon was that while in prison, a yellow fever epidemic had broken out and Mudd had saved many prisoners' and guards' lives.

Dr. Mudd, by the way, was an ancestor of TV newsman Roger Mudd.

"I Would Rather Be Right Than Be President"

Poor Henry Clay of Kentucky was one of the more tragic figures in presidential election history.

Clay was a brilliant man and a leading statesman for more than forty years. He was one of the most powerful men in the U.S. Senate. He desperately wanted to be president, but failed on five different occasions. Twice he didn't get the nomination he sought (in 1828 and 1836), and three times he was nominated but lost the election (in 1824 to John

Quincy Adams, in 1832 to Andrew Jackson, and in 1844 to James Polk).

In each case, Clay took some unpopular stands that cost him votes, but that he thought were correct. When told by a fellow congressman that some of his views were preventing him from winning elections, Clay, who so wanted the presidency, made his famous, poignant quote, "Sir, I would rather be right than be president." Sadly, his wish was granted.

First Father and Son

John Harrison was never a U.S. president—but he's the only man in history whose dad *and* son were both presidents.

His father was the ninth U.S. president, William Henry Harrison, elected in 1840. His son was the twenty-third president, Benjamin Harrison, elected in 1888.

John's main occupation was farming, and while he never made it to the top political office, he did serve as a U.S. congressman from Ohio from 1852 to 1857.

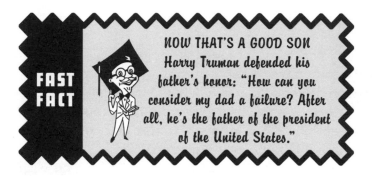

FAST FACT

NOW THAT'S A GOOD SON
Harry Truman defended his father's honor: "How can you consider my dad a failure? After all, he's the father of the president of the United States."

The First Woman

Senator Margaret Chase Smith of Maine made history when her name was placed in nomination for president of the United States at the Republican convention in 1964.

Though this was the first time a woman was put in nomination for president by a major party, this wasn't the first first for Smith: She had already achieved political fame as the first woman ever elected to both houses of Congress. Maine voters had sent her to the U.S. House of Representatives for four terms, and then to the U.S. Senate for three terms in the 1940s, '50s, and '60s.

The time seemed ripe to nominate a woman for president—the women's movement was just getting started in the U.S., and Smith was generally well-respected by her colleagues in the Republican Party. But Barry Goldwater was the leading candidate, and only one ballot was taken at the convention.

Smith managed to get twenty-seven votes. She and others in the field (William Scranton, Nelson Rockefeller, and George Romney) were overwhelmed by Goldwater, who got 883 votes on that first ballot and won the Republican nomination. Nevertheless, Smith made her mark.

The American Dream

Millard Fillmore's story is the stuff that movies are made of. Born to a poor family in upstate New York, Fillmore had to seek jobs as a youngster to help support his parents and eight brothers and sisters. He had little formal schooling and, even by the age of fourteen, was barely able to read.

But Fillmore decided then to make something of himself. There's a famous story that he got hold of a dictionary and studied it every day in order to learn to read better. Other books followed, and Fillmore began a program of intense self-education.

By age twenty-eight he won election to the New York House of Representatives and five years later was elected to the U.S. Congress. By age forty-six, this man who could hardly read at age fourteen had become chancellor of the University of Buffalo. Two years later he was nominated for U.S. vice president under Zachary Taylor. They were elected—and when Taylor died in office, Millard Fillmore became president of the United States. Talk about pulling yourself up by your bootstraps. That's a real success story!

Duel to the Death

Andrew Jackson, the seventh U.S. president, was a rough, tough man who grew up in the late 1700s in the then-frontier life of the Carolinas and Tennessee, among people who were ready to fight at any time. Jackson fought many duels in his life, but one stands out from the rest—the famous, well-publicized pistol duel when he was thirty-nine years old against a man regarded as one of the best shots in the country.

The man, Charles Dickinson, made insulting sexual comments about Jackson's wife, Rachel, who had married Jackson before her divorce from her first husband was official. Jackson felt compelled to defend his wife's honor, so he challenged Dickinson to a duel in which they would stand twenty-four feet apart and fire at each other.

Jackson's shot was right on target; he killed Dickinson. Dickinson's shot grazed Jackson's chest and broke two ribs, but Jackson survived. The famous dueler became president at age sixty-one, and lived to the ripe age of seventy-eight.

A Sudden Chill

While at his summer home on Campobello Island in New Brunswick, Canada, in 1921—eleven years before he would be elected president—Franklin Roosevelt became chilled while swimming. The next day he found he could not stand or even move his arms or legs. No, this wasn't just some bad dream; Roosevelt had become paralyzed from polio. Although he eventually would regain use of his hands, he was unable to walk unaided for the rest of his life. But this didn't seem to slow him down.

Roosevelt's disability was fairly well hidden from

the public during his presidency. He was almost never shown being helped to stand or walk. Roosevelt was most often pictured while sitting down, and the press and photo corps rarely mentioned or showed any difficulties he had.

In those days before TV was a mass medium, there were people in the nation who were not even aware that their president couldn't walk unaided. And even if they did know, would it have mattered?

There's No Place Like Home

Remember that old saying that no prophet is welcome in his hometown? Well, you could say it was true of Franklin Roosevelt, one of America's most famous presidents.

Roosevelt was popular across the nation. He was the only person elected president four times and each time he won by a comfortable margin. And yet, he never carried his home county, Dutchess County in New York. In each of his four elections, a majority of the home folks voted for Roosevelt's opponent.

It's not that Roosevelt was a bad kid that the neighbors refused to forgive. Instead, the reason had to do with voter registration: Dutchess County was largely Republican, and Roosevelt was a Democrat. And not even hometown allegiance could overcome that difference.

Lost in the Mail

In 1847, the Whigs, then a major political party, nominated military hero Zachary Taylor to run for president. It was a tremendous honor, one that Taylor, shockingly, almost didn't know about.

During the nomination process, Taylor was at an army post. There was, of course, no telephone, radio, or TV in those days, and telegraph lines did not yet reach Louisiana, where Taylor was stationed, so the Whigs sent Taylor a letter telling him of his nomination. Taylor refused to accept the letter and didn't open it. Why? Because the letter came postage due, and Taylor didn't want to pay for it. But it's not as if the Whigs forgot the stamp. You see, back then it was customary for the receiver, not the sender, of mail to pay the postage. And Taylor wasn't cheap, but as a famous general, he received a lot of unsolicited mail and made it policy not to pay for letters. So Taylor didn't know he was nominated to run for president of the United States until the Whigs sent a messenger to tell him.

All's well that ends well: Taylor ran for president and won.

Famous Four

We have sculptor Gutzon Borglum to thank for the enormous carved portraits of U.S. presidents that decorate Mt. Rushmore in the Black Hills of South Dakota. He started the work of carving the presidential faces in 1927. The job wasn't completed until 1941. The massive faces are each about sixty feet high.

But how were the presidents selected for this amazing honor? Borglum himself chose the honorees: George Washington, Thomas Jefferson, Abraham Lincoln, and Theodore Roosevelt. The first three seem an obvious choice, as they are typically considered to be some of our greatest presidents. So how did Teddy Roosevelt get into that gang? Not that there's anything wrong with T. Roosevelt, but he is usually not mentioned in the same echelon of presidents as Washington, Jefferson, and Lincoln. The answer is simple. He happened to be a favorite of Borglum. Maybe it was the mustache.

> Gutzon Borglum's son couldn't have been better named for the task of finishing Mt. Rushmore after his father's death. His name? Lincoln.

FAST FACT

From the Big House to the White House

Bet you didn't think someone could run for president from prison, but it's true. Incredibly, during the 1920 presidential election, one of the men running for the highest office in the land was at the same time serving a ten-year sentence in a federal penitentiary.

That year the election pitted a third-party Socialist candidate, Eugene Debs, against Republican Warren Harding and Democrat James Cox. Debs may have been free to enter the race, but he wasn't free to do much else. Convicted in 1918 of violating the Espionage Act (because he'd opposed America's entry in World War I), Debs was locked up in the Atlanta Penitentiary during the entire presidential campaign.

Harding won that famous election with over sixteen million votes. Cox finished second with over nine million. Debs, sitting in his prison cell, got 919,799 votes.

A year after Harding took office, he commuted Debs's sentence. Debs lived another six years and wrote a book, *Walls and Bars*, about prison conditions.

But What if Debs Had Won?

The fact that Eugene Debs got as many votes as he did made people begin to wonder how a man in jail could serve as president of the country. Just imagine the challenges of trying to run the nation from a barred cell, not to mention the wardrobe limitations!

Strangely, there's apparently nothing specific in the Constitution prohibiting such a development. There's nothing about morality or character or even conviction of a crime. The Constitution does address presidential death, resignation, and "inability to discharge the powers and duties of the office." That last clause might apply to a person in prison, but experts aren't sure.

Before the 1920 election, there wasn't much discussion about what would happen if Debs won because almost no one gave him any kind of chance. But when he got almost one million votes, some lawmakers wondered if a Constitutional amendment should be considered. There was talk for a while, but the issue died down and nothing was ever done. Stay tuned!

Rub-a-dub-dub, Prez Stuck in a Tub

William Howard Taft weighed as much as 350 pounds when he was in the White House. Taft was so big that he found the bathtub there—and probably the bathtubs everywhere—too small.

Poor, big Taft got stuck in the tub one day, and had to call for aides to pull him out. Sadly, reports say that this humbling moment happened more than once.

Finally, someone took some initiative and ordered a larger bathtub. The bathtub was so big that four workmen sat in it to have their picture taken. Wonder how Taft felt about that. . . .

Get It in Writing

The story of Pierre L'Enfant, a French architect who settled in America in the late 1700s, teaches us an important lesson: Always get it in writing. In 1791, L'Enfant, who is considered the first modern city planner, was chosen to design the layout for the new American capital of Washington, D.C.

He created Washington's famous rectangular and diagonal streets and planned for malls, impressive public buildings, and parks in what many consider a beautiful city.

But L'Enfant's personality apparently irritated members of Congress and even President Washington, who fired him before his work was completed. Unfortunately for L'Enfant, his fee had not been agreed to in advance. When he submitted his bill for more than $95,000, it didn't go over very well. Congress made several compromise offers for less money, but L'Enfant wouldn't bargain. Finally, in anger, Congress voted to pay him just $1,300. L'Enfant went into bankruptcy, then spent years trying to get more money from Congress, but never did. He died in poverty.

Congress eventually tried to make it up to Monsieur L'Enfant—too little, too late—by erecting a monument to him in Arlington National Cemetery in 1909, eighty-four years after his death. Though his monument overlooks the city he designed, he probably would have preferred the cash.

Thanks to a young woman's question during a 1992 appearance on MTV, the nation learned Bill Clinton's underwear preference. (It's briefs, in case you're wondering.)

FAST FACT

One of These Things is Not Like the Other

Every U.S. president throughout history has either been a member of Congress, a governor of a state, a famous army general, or served in a high-level government job. All except for one: Chester Arthur.

For someone with a pretty average background, Arthur made it to the presidency on something of dumb luck. He had held a government job, but it was a minor one, as a collector for the Port of New York, where he supervised the collection of import duties. And he was ultimately fired from that job when a new administration took over.

Arthur also practiced law off and on, and worked for the Republican Party. It was in the latter capacity that Arthur became a delegate to the Republican convention in 1880. That year the convention nominated James Garfield to run for president, instead of an early favorite, Ulysses Grant. Arthur was part of the circle that supported Grant, and party insiders, looking for Grant supporters to balance the ticket, chose him to run as vice president despite the fact that he was practically unknown.

Garfield-Arthur won the election. But Garfield was assassinated early in his first term, and the former duty collector found himself president of the United States.

Claim to Fame

The only thing most folks knew about Vice President Chester Arthur when he became president upon President Garfield's assassination in 1881 was his nickname. He was known as "The Man with Three First Names," because his full name was Chester Alan Arthur.

Despite his lack of national experience when Arthur assumed the presidency, he was given credit for reforming Civil Service, and was also fairly popular. However, when he tried to get his party's

1884 nomination to run for a second term, he was turned aside. He died a year later.

Losers Usually Don't Come Back to Win

Of all the men who've been nominated by a major party to run for president in the last 100 years, only *one* who lost an election came back later to win a presidential election.

Can you guess who that one man was?

If you guessed Richard Nixon, you'd be right. He ran against John Kennedy in 1960 and lost, then ran against Hubert Humphrey in 1968, and won.

To find a comparable situation, you'd have to go back more than 100 years, when Grover Cleveland lost to Benjamin Harrison in 1888, then ran against Harrison in 1892 and won.

GETTING THE WORD OUT...
KDKA, Pittsburgh, the world's first commercial radio station, became the first to broadcast presidential election returns on November 2, 1920.

FAST FACT

A Friend in Need

When William McKinley was governor of Ohio in the early 1890s, he cosigned a loan for a tin plate manufacturer for $100,000 (in 1890s dollars). The business failed, and the bank demanded $100,000 from McKinley. McKinley didn't have it and was threatened with bankruptcy.

The future looked bleak until Mark Hanna, a millionaire political kingmaker from Cleveland, came to the rescue. Hanna paid off McKinley's debt—and went a step further. He wanted to make McKinley president of the United States.

Hanna opened a drive to get McKinley the Republican nomination in 1896. He raised a then-record $3.5 million in campaign funds, and used his clout within the party to influence delegates at the national convention. McKinley not only got the nomination but Hanna's friend, New Jersey state senator Garret Hobart, was chosen as the vice presidential candidate. The ticket won in November and Hanna had both his men in the White House.

From the Front Porch

William McKinley's wife, Ida, was an invalid for many

years and was also prone to epileptic fits. When McKinley ran for president in 1896, he promised his wife he would not leave her side to make campaign trips around the country.

McKinley kept his word and stayed home in Canton, Ohio. This might have spelled doom for most candidates, but not for McKinley. Over the next several months, his backers brought thousands of visitors to the front lawn of his house. McKinley stood on his porch and gave his speeches.

The press dubbed it "The Front Porch" campaign, and it worked. McKinley won the election over the colorful William Jennings Bryan, who had been active on the campaign trail.

McKinley got almost one million more votes than Bryan, and he and Ida soon left their Canton home for the White House. Think McKinley delivered speeches from the White House porch for old times' sake?

A Presidential Wedding Party

When Eleanor Roosevelt married Franklin Roosevelt, she didn't have to think twice about changing her monogrammed towels or passport. That's because her maiden name was Roosevelt, too!

Eleanor was a distant cousin of Franklin—and would become the only first lady whose maiden name was the same as her husband's last name.

But Eleanor was an even closer relative of another president: Her father's older brother was Theodore Roosevelt. Uncle Theodore came to Eleanor's rescue when she was about to wed Franklin in 1904. Eleanor's father was already dead, so she asked her uncle Theodore, then serving as president, to come to New York City for the ceremony and walk her down the aisle. Theodore agreed—and in so doing, created a wedding party that consisted of a current president, a future president, and a future first lady.

Mrs. President?

Did you know that the term "first lady," a name for the president's wife, was not used during the first 100 years of U.S. history?

It all began in 1877 when a popular play was produced about Dolley Madison, the wife of the fourth president, James Madison. The play's title was *The First Lady of the Land*.

Rutherford Hayes was president at the time the play opened. The press started calling his wife, Lucy, "the first lady," and the tradition was born.

Of all forty-two U.S. presidents through George W. Bush's first term, only eleven have served two full four-year terms.

FAST FACT

Just Shy

George Washington did a lot of things. But though he was elected twice and completed his second term, George did not serve a full eight years.

Why? Because Washington's intended inauguration day for his first term was pushed back from March 4, 1789 to April 30. Government officials weren't holding out for better weather, they were still just trying to get organized.

It's because of this delay that Washington's presidency was fifty-seven days short of eight years. If only the government had gotten its act together, Washington could have added yet another achievement to his résumé!

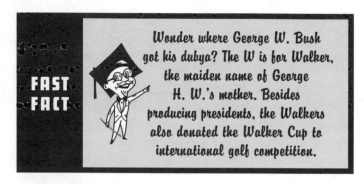

FAST FACT

Wonder where George W. Bush got his dubya? The W is for Walker, the maiden name of George H. W.'s mother. Besides producing presidents, the Walkers also donated the Walker Cup to international golf competition.

Pulitzer Presidents

Can you guess which one of our presidents was a Pulitzer Prize–winning author?

The answer is John Kennedy. Kennedy was just twenty-three years old when he penned a book about England's slow response to the coming of World War II. The book, titled *Why England Slept*, was an expansion of his senior thesis at Harvard. It sold well, but didn't win any awards, let alone the Pulitzer.

Kennedy went on from there to work as a foreign correspondent for the International News Service, and while still in his thirties, began writing a book about heroic deeds of political figures. He called it *Profiles in Courage*. It was that book that earned Kennedy the Pulitzer Prize for biography in 1957—three years before he became president.

AND THE WINNER IS . . .
VIRGINIA!
Eight presidents were born in Virginia, more than any other state. Ohio's a close second with seven and New York is third with four.

FAST FACT

You Just Never Know

Ulysses S. Grant is practically the poster child for late bloomers. As a young adult, he tried farming and failed. He worked in real estate and failed. He ran a store and failed. He joined the U.S. Army and was discharged for alcoholism.

Things were looking bleak for the then thirty-nine-year-old Grant. It was 1861, the year the Civil War began. President Lincoln called for volunteers and Grant decided to reenter the army. Although he had been a less-than- average student during his college days at West Point, his military training and bold moves with his troops served him well. Grant garnered victory after victory in the Civil War.

Despite reports that Grant was drinking heavily again, he became a favorite of Lincoln, who eventually promoted him to top command of all Union armies.

He led final battles of the war, and accepted Robert E. Lee's ultimate surrender at Appomattox, Virginia.

Grant became a popular choice for president. He won the 1868 presidential election and was reelected four years later, capping a spectacular rise from failure to success.

What a Difference a Mistake Can Make

The man we know as Ulysses S. Grant was actually born Hiram Ulysses Grant. But when he applied to West Point, the congressman who recommended him made an error on the application, listing his name as Ulysses Simpson Grant. The congressman put "Ulysses" first because that's what his parents called him and he came up with "Simpson" from Grant's mother's maiden name.

Grant was happy with the error because he didn't much like the initials—HUG—of his original name. He never bothered to correct the congressman's mistake and it was a good thing, too, because that mistake helped launch Grant's success.

As Ulysses S. Grant in the Civil War, he demanded unconditional surrender of Southern forces. The public took his two new first initials and gave him the nickname of "Unconditional Surrender Grant"—a name that helped him get elected president. Go, U.S.!

WORKING FROM HOME
Did you realize that the leader of the United States works from home?

FAST FACT

I Don't Care *How* Old You Are . . .

Sara Delano was not a lady to be messed with. She came from an extremely wealthy family and married a wealthy man, James Roosevelt. And even though their son, Franklin, grew up to be president of the United States, this did not stop Sara from trying to dominate her son's life. When Franklin was young, Sara made him live by a rigid schedule, setting specific times when he should study and when he could play. She was never shy about telling him what to do—even when he was governor, and later president. But Franklin openly defied his mother when he picked his bride. Sara did not want another woman in Franklin's life, and she especially disliked his choice of a distant cousin, Eleanor Roosevelt. Franklin went ahead and married Eleanor anyway.

As you might imagine, Sara made life difficult for Eleanor. One particularly telling anecdote of her controlling ways took place while Eleanor and Franklin were on their honeymoon. Sara rented a house for the new couple and furnished it completely to her own tastes. Eleanor was upset to learn she could not decorate her own home.

Until Sara's death in 1941—eight years into Franklin's presidency and thirty-six years into their marriage—Franklin and Eleanor often felt Sara's interference in their lives. Franklin was a grown man running the nation, but in his mother's mind, he was still just her little boy.

A True Role Model

Eleanor Roosevelt had many advantages: She was from the prestigious Roosevelt family, she grew up in wealth, and she married into wealth. But things weren't always easy, and Eleanor suffered many indignities throughout her life. There was her domineering mother-in-law who disliked her, the known infidelities of her husband, and the cruel jokes made about her by the public when she was first lady.

Nonetheless, Eleanor was determined to overcome her personal problems and make a career of distinguished public service. She campaigned for equal rights for women, minorities, and the underprivileged. She wrote a widely syndicated newspaper column, "My Day," and after her husband's death, became a delegate to the United Nations and was elected chairwoman of the U.N. Human Rights Commission.

In her later years, Eleanor had turned her life from one of scorn and ridicule to popular respect, and was voted one of the most admired women in the world. One of her favorite mottoes was: "No one can make you feel inferior without your consent." Hear, hear, Eleanor!

POPULOUS, BUT NOT VERY PRESIDENTIAL California, which today has the largest population of any U.S. state, is the birthplace of only one president: Richard Nixon.

FAST FACT

The Name Game

When George Washington was president, the two main political parties weren't called Democrats or Republicans. The parties then were the Federalists and Anti-Federalists.

The Federalists stood for a strong central government, while the Anti-Federalists wanted more power for the states. George Washington was a Federalist, as was the second president, John Adams.

Meanwhile, Thomas Jefferson was an Anti-Federalist, but he changed the name of his party to Democratic-Republican, and that's what it was called when he served as the third president. Eventually, the Democrat-Republicans altered their name again and became the Democratic Party. They held the White House from 1801 to 1841, when the unlikely named Whigs took over. Got it?

It Has Nothing to Do With Hair

The Whig party elected their first president, William Henry Harrison, in 1840. The Whigs got their name not because they wore wigs but from an old Scottish party called the Whiggamores.

The Scottish word *Wiggamore* described those opposed to the ruling party in England. In the U.S., when a new major party was being formed in the 1830s to oppose the platforms of the incumbent Democrats, they chose a shortened version of Whiggamore, became Whigs, and put four presidents in the White House—Harrison, John Tyler, Zachary Taylor, and Millard Fillmore.

After Fillmore's unpopular presidency, the Whigs never again elected another president. They faded away when a new party, the Republicans, came along with their first president, Abraham Lincoln. Since then every president has been either a Democrat or a Republican, and the Federalists, Anti-Federalists, and Whigs are just a memory.

Although he failed to win the electoral vote, Al Gore had the second highest number of popular votes of all time. Ronald Reagan holds the record—he received the most.

FAST FACT

From Schoolhouse to White House

Lyndon Johnson was an industrious one. At age nineteen, to get enough money to attend Southwest Texas State Teachers College, he took odd jobs as a janitor, shoe-shine man, grape picker, and auto mechanic, and borrowed seventy-five dollars from a bank. After graduation, he earned a teacher's certificate and began a career as a schoolteacher.

Far from the White House, Johnson taught grade school in the little town of Cotulla, Texas, and then moved to Sam Houston High School in Houston. While still teaching, Johnson entered politics, campaigning in 1931, at age twenty-three, for Congressman Richard Kleberg. Kleberg owned the famous King Ranch, the biggest ranch in Texas (it was about the size of the entire state of Rhode Island). Kleberg took a liking to Johnson and brought him to Washington as his secretary. This was Johnson's lucky break. He learned how to operate in Washington, and the ex-schoolteacher went on to a career as a congressman himself, a senator, vice president, and ultimately president.

FAST FACT

Great oranges, but no presidents: No president was ever born in Florida.

The Kitchen Cabinet

Ever notice at parties how everyone tends to congregate in the kitchen? Well, the White House is no exception. Andrew Jackson actually often ignored his official cabinet and instead met with a bunch of cronies and advisers in, you guessed it, the White House kitchen.

The group—called his Kitchen Cabinet—was a collection of old army friends, newspaper people, and assorted politicians. Jackson enjoyed meeting with them, and at times, they had more influence on the president than his official cabinet did.

But why did Jackson ignore his official cabinet? Blame it on a woman named Margaret O'Neale. Ms. O'Neale lived with her family in a combination of a tavern and inn that they owned in Washington. She was staying with her family while her husband, a navy purser, was away at sea. Jackson wasn't involved with Ms. O'Neale, but another resident of the inn was . . .

Senator John Eaton, a friend of President Jackson's from his home state of Tennessee, was a resident of the inn, and had taken a liking to Ms. O'Neale. In 1828, Ms. O'Neale's husband died at sea. A year later, she married Senator Eaton.

That same year, President Jackson chose Senator Eaton to be his secretary of war—a choice that was not welcomed by other members of Jackson's official cabinet, or their wives. There had been gossip about the relationship between the senator and Ms. O'Neale before their marriage, and some looked down upon Ms. O'Neale because her father ran a tavern.

Jackson stood by Eaton, but his cabinet was badly divided, with some members in support of Jackson and Eaton, and others opposed. The turmoil within the cabinet caused Jackson, a rough, tough, old army man, to turn to his friends in his Kitchen Cabinet with whom he felt more comfortable anyway.

Winners, Losers, and Revenge

It's hard to believe, but four times in the history of U.S. presidential elections, the candidate with the most popular votes has lost the election. Blame it on the Electoral College system.

In 1824, Andrew Jackson got more popular votes than John Quincy Adams (647,286 to 508,064), but Adams became president. (Jackson got revenge four years later in a rematch with Adams when Jackson won both the popular and electoral votes.) In 1876, Samuel Tilden got more popular votes than

Rutherford Hayes (4,300,590 to 4,036,298), but Hayes became president. In 1888, Grover Cleveland topped Benjamin Harrison in popular votes (5,540,309 to 5,444,337), but Harrison won the election. (Cleveland turned the tables on Harrison in the next election.) And in 2000, Al Gore got more popular votes than George W. Bush (51,003,894 to 50,459,211), but Bush became president.

Just like Mom used to say, popularity is not everything!

Mary Todd Lincoln didn't call her husband sweetie or honey or even Abe . . . instead, she called him Mr. Lincoln.

FAST FACT

Out-of-Town Oath

A total of six U.S. presidents were sworn into office in a place other than Washington, D.C.

George Washington took the oath for his first term in what was then the nation's capital: New York City. By the time his second-term inauguration had rolled around, the capital had been moved to Philadelphia, and that's where Washington took the oath for that term, as did John Adams when it was his turn.

The other four presidents who took the oath away from Washington D.C. had been vice presidents when they were suddenly thrust into the presidency upon the death of the president.

Chester Arthur was home in New York City when President Garfield died, and he took the oath there. Theodore Roosevelt was in Buffalo, New York, when President McKinley died, and went to the private home of a friend for the swearing in. Calvin Coolidge was at his home in Plymouth, Vermont, when President Harding died. Lyndon Johnson was in Dallas when President Kennedy was assassinated and he was sworn in there.

Harding's Scandals

President Warren Harding had it tough. His secretary of the interior, Albert Fall, was convicted of accepting a bribe and sent to prison—and that was only one of the scandals that rocked Harding's administration.

Fall was involved in the notorious Teapot Dome affair. He gave government-owned oil leases for land in Teapot Dome, Wyoming, and Elk Hills, California, to two men in return for a payment of $400,000 that he kept for himself.

In the meantime, Harding's attorney general, Harry Daugherty, was charged in a separate case concerning his administration of the Alien Property Custodian's Office. Daugherty faced two trials and was acquitted, but a colleague, accused of arranging settlements for Daugherty's office, committed suicide.

And as if that weren't enough, a lawyer for the Veterans' Bureau, charged with misuse of funds, also committed suicide, while the director of the agency went to jail.

Some suspect that a broken heart, caused by his friends' betrayals, was the true cause of Harding's illness and death in 1923.

FAST FACT

A Dubious Honor

Richard Nixon was in hot water. With the scandal of the Watergate break-in and cover-up engulfing his second term, he resisted calls for his resignation. But one summer day in 1974, all that changed. For it was on that day that several Republican congressional leaders who had been his staunch defenders called on him at the White House.

Led by Senator Barry Goldwater and Representative John Rhodes, they told him his support in Congress had deteriorated and that he faced certain impeachment. The next day, August 9, Nixon announced his resignation, and earned the dubious honor of becoming the first president ever to resign his office.

Nixon lived another twenty years. He died in 1994 at the age of eighty-one.

FAST FACT

George Washington, one of the most popular and respected presidents ever, was not above suspicion: Some suspected that he overdrew his presidential salary.

The Year with Two Thanksgivings

It sounds like the beginning of some child's fantasy, but in truth, there was once a year with two

Thanksgivings. In 1939, President Franklin Roosevelt thought it would help the economy if he advanced Thanksgiving from the traditional fourth Thursday of November to the third Thursday to allow a longer Christmas shopping season.

The trouble was that twenty-four of the then forty-eight states refused to go along, and kept the holiday on the fourth Thursday. And the other twenty-four states accepted Roosevelt's proposal and celebrated it the week before. The confusion did not go over well. So the next year, Roosevelt abandoned the idea and the entire country had Thanksgiving on the same day.

Congress finally made it official in 1941, when it passed a law declaring Thanksgiving would be celebrated on the fourth Thursday of November. Since then, the entire nation has celebrated—and given thanks—as one.

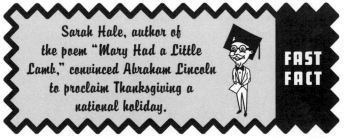

Sarah Hale, author of the poem "Mary Had a Little Lamb," convinced Abraham Lincoln to proclaim Thanksgiving a national holiday.

FAST FACT

Norfolk County's Three Famous Johns

Presidents Kennedy and the two Adamses share a few similarities. They're not only all named John, but all three were born in Norfolk County, Massachusetts. John Adams and John Quincy Adams were born in the Boston suburb of Quincy, and John Kennedy was born in the Boston suburb of Brookline.

Mind Over Matter

Teddy Roosevelt was an impressive example of mind over matter. As a sickly child, Roosevelt suffered from asthma and other frequent illnesses, but he was determined to have, as he put it, a strong body and mind. He took up hiking, swimming, horseback riding, and boxing. He believed in what he called "the strenuous life," and he became one of the most active men ever to reach the presidency.

But when Roosevelt was in the White House, one of these activities cost him dearly.

Roosevelt challenged a military aide to a boxing match, and during the match one of the aide's punches severely damaged Roosevelt's left eye. Roosevelt lost sight completely in that eye for the rest of his life. He had never had good eyesight to begin with. As a child, kids teased him about not being able to read signs or see objects that they could. Roosevelt was diagnosed with an acute case of nearsightedness, and he began wearing glasses at an early age. But his poor eyesight never kept him from his "strenuous life," or a successful presidency.

The Stay-at-Home Presidents

It seems barely a week goes by without the president boarding Air Force One, but did you know that from George Washington in 1789 through William McKinley in 1901, no president ever set foot outside the country? The first president to leave the U.S. while in office was Theodore Roosevelt, who visited the site of the Panama Canal in 1906.

The Power of One

Have you ever wondered if it's really true that every vote counts? For proof there's no need to look any further than the story of President Andrew Johnson's impeachment. President Johnson was the first to be impeached, in 1868. He wasn't guilty of any moral or criminal charge, but had defied a former act of Congress that said a president could not remove a cabinet officer without Senate approval.

Johnson believed the act was an unjustified attempt by Congress to limit the power of the presidency during controversies surrounding the Reconstruction after the Civil War. So Johnson went ahead and dismissed a man he disagreed with, Secretary of War Edwin Stanton, without notifying the Senate. Some members of Congress who were already displeased with Johnson were outraged by that so-called illegal dismissal. They saw it as their chance to remove Johnson and began impeachment proceedings.

At Johnson's impeachment trial, thirty-five senators voted him guilty, and nineteen voted not guilty. A two-thirds vote is necessary for conviction, so by the slim margin of just one vote Johnson was acquitted and allowed to finish out his term as president.

History Repeats Itself, Sort Of

In 1998, for the second time in U.S. history, the House

of Representatives voted to impeach a president. The House charged Bill Clinton with perjury and obstruction of justice in the attempt to cover up an alleged sexual relationship with the former White House intern Monica Lewinsky.

But history repeated itself, and just as with the first impeachment of President Johnson, Clinton was acquitted by the Senate. His perjury charge drew forty-five (of 100) votes for conviction, and the obstruction charge drew fifty. Since sixty-seven, or two-thirds, were necessary for conviction, Clinton was free to remain president.

So how does the impeachment process work? Under the Constitution, only the House may vote for impeachment, which is a charge and *not* a conviction. Then the Senate conducts the trial on the charges and decides whether the president shall be convicted and removed from office, or acquitted and allowed to stay.

The Quiet Guy Pipes Up

Calvin Coolidge was known for his verbal reticence. But on a few occasions this notoriously tight-lipped leader had some words of wisdom.

Coolidge drew national attention and built a reputation for himself during his term as governor of Massachusetts, when the Boston police force threatened to strike. In a memorable speech, Coolidge stated, "There is no right to strike against the public safety by anybody, anywhere, any time."

Later, when Coolidge became president, he was outspoken about another issue as well. Openly pro-business, Coolidge famously quipped, "The business of America is business." Certainly some CEOs would agree!

FAST FACT

Anything goes... Humorist Will Rogers said of Coolidge, who was a supporter of laissez-faire during the Roaring Twenties, "He didn't do nothing, and that's what we wanted done."

Oh, Say Can You See . . .

These days, if you go to almost any high school, college, or professional baseball, football, basketball, or hockey game, an announcer will induce the crowd to rise, stating, "Ladies and gentlemen, our national anthem." But if you had gone to such an event before 1931, you wouldn't have heard those words at all. For although "The Star-Spangled Banner" was written in 1814, it did not become the national anthem of the United States until 117 years later, in 1931, when Herbert Hoover signed the bill that gave the song its official status.

In all the years before that, the U.S. did not have an official national anthem!

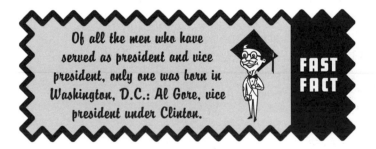

Of all the men who have served as president and vice president, only one was born in Washington, D.C.: Al Gore, vice president under Clinton.

FAST FACT

0 for 3

Many candidates have run for president over the years on tickets that were not part of the two mainstream parties—but no third-party candidate has ever won.

Ross Perot got the most votes when he ran on the Reform Party ticket against Democrat Bill Clinton and

Republican George H. W. Bush in 1992. But even though more than nineteen million Americans voted for Perot, he still finished a distant third to Clinton's forty-four million and Bush's thirty-nine million votes.

Only one third-party candidate ever finished second. In 1912, four years after leaving the White House at the end of his second term, Theodore Roosevelt ran for president as the Progressive or Bull Moose Party candidate. He beat Republican William Howard Taft by four million votes to three million, but Democrat Woodrow Wilson won the election with more than eight million votes.

(Curious about the name of the Bull Moose Party? It came from Roosevelt himself, who said at the beginning of his campaign that he felt like a bull moose—ready for action.)

The "Know Nothings" and Other Third Parties

Former Whig president Millard Fillmore tried to get back to the White House in 1856. He didn't win, but maybe the name of his party was partially to blame. Called the Know Nothing Party, it was anti-immigration and anti-Catholic and began as a secret society. The name came from party members' infamous responses to questions about what happened at their meetings—ever secretive, they would always respond, "I don't know."

The Know Nothings were more formally known as the American Party, and share their third-party status with such groups as the Free Soil Party in 1848 (anti-slavery), the Greenback Party in 1876 (pro financial reform), the Prohibition Party in 1884 (anti-liquor), the Socialist Party in the early 1900s (labor rights), the Progressive Party in 1924 (farmer and labor rights), the Dixiecrats in 1948 (segregationists), the American Independent Party in 1968 (states' rights), and Ralph Nader's Green Party in 2000 (environmental and corporate power concerns).

Each of these parties has had its followers, and some influenced the outcome of elections by taking votes away from mainstream candidates, but none ever came close to winning in its own right. But who knows what the future holds?

Though no president from 1789 to 1961 served in the U.S. Navy, the next five consecutive presidents after 1961 were all navy men.

FAST FACT

World War Commanders— Without Service

What does it take to be commander in chief? Surprisingly, you don't need actual military experience . . . you just have to be president. Though well over half of all U.S. presidents performed active service at some point in their lives, the two presidents who led the nation in World Wars I and II never did. Although they led the country during the great wars, neither Woodrow Wilson nor Franklin Roosevelt had had any prior military experience.

Article II, Section 2 of the Constitution says, "The President shall be the Commander in Chief of the Army and Navy of the United States, and of the Militia of the several States, when called into the actual Service of the United States."

And speaking of that article, notice anything missing? There's no mention of the air force or the marines. It's not that the direction of those groups falls to someone else, it's just that those branches of the military didn't exist when the Constitution was written. Thus there's no mention of them in the Constitution—and there's never been an amendment to take care of the omission.

One last note: Presidents can do a lot of things as commander in chief, but they cannot declare war.

Article I, Section 8 of the Constitution specifically gives that power to Congress.

Off to a Slow Start

Every presidential election in U.S. history has taken place in an even-numbered year—except one. The first election could not be held until the Constitution was declared in effect, and that happened in 1789 instead of the anticipated 1788. So George Washington was elected in 1789. The country got back on track, though, and the next election was held in 1792. And since then, the U.S. has had a presidential election every four years like clockwork.

Speeding Up the Process

Presidents used to be inaugurated on March 4, until the November presidential election in 1936, when the inauguration was moved to the following January 20.

Why? It wasn't because the president wanted to show off his winter wardrobe. Congress finally realized that waiting until March to inaugurate a new president was too long a time between the November election and the March inauguration: Lame duck presidents were in office four whole months before the end of their term.

So January 20 was picked as the ideal date. It would give a new president enough time to organize his staff and reduce the lame duck period of the outgoing president.

That's all well and good, but whose decision was it to hold the inauguration outside in the cold?

The Foreign-Born First Lady

The Constitution says that all presidents must be born in America, but there is no rule on first ladies. Still, of all the first ladies in U.S. history as of 2004, only one was born outside our land.

Who was this foreign-born first lady? She was born in England, her name was Louisa, and she was the wife of President John Quincy Adams.

The Woman Behind the Trees

We have Helen Taft to thank for the beautiful cherry

trees planted along the Tidal Basin. Helen, the wife of President William Howard Taft, had spent time in Asia and especially admired Japanese cherry trees. When she was first lady, in 1909, she asked the mayor of Tokyo to send some trees to Washington. He did—but, sadly, they were burned by the Department of Agriculture, who found them to be diseased.

The good mayor, disappointed by the fate of his gift, sent three thousand more trees. The Department of Agriculture gave these trees a clean bill of health and they were promptly planted along the Tidal Basin in Washington by order of Mrs. Taft.

Every spring since then, thousands of tourists come to see the cherry blossoms in bloom and enjoy this wonderful gift.

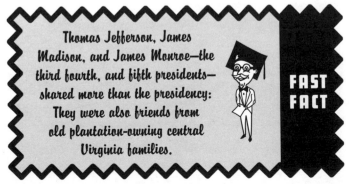

Thomas Jefferson, James Madison, and James Monroe—the third, fourth, and fifth presidents—shared more than the presidency: They were also friends from old plantation-owning central Virginia families.

FAST FACT

From Diamond to Oval

George H. W. Bush was a lanky lefthander when he played first base for the Yale University baseball team in 1947.

Bush was elected captain and led them to a baseball first. The first-ever College World Series was held in 1947, and Bush's Yale squad was good enough to qualify for that initial postseason college event. They reached the finals, but lost to the University of California at Berkeley 8–7 in the deciding game.

Bush was already a family man by then. He had been married for two years, and at the time of the College World Series, had a one-year-old son who shared his first name. Little did anyone know then that the lanky lefthander and his young son would both go on to become president of the United States.

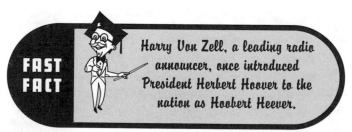

FAST FACT

Harry Von Zell, a leading radio announcer, once introduced President Herbert Hoover to the nation as Hoobert Heever.

A Tragic Tale

In the 1872 election, Republican Ulysses Grant ran for his second term as president against Democrat Horace Greeley. Greeley was a well-known newspaper publisher and editor who achieved fame by popularizing the catchphrase for western expansion: "Go west, young man." (Greeley used the phrase in a New York *Tribune* editorial, imploring unemployed New Yorkers to seek opportunities in the fast-growing western part of the country.)

During his presidential campaign in the fall of 1872, Greeley became ill. Unfortunately, his wife was suffering from an illness at the same time. And on top of that, Greeley faced personal financial problems.

In late October, Greeley's wife died. On November 4, election day, Greeley lost to Grant, and on November 29, Greeley died. So even if he had won, he never would have served.

It was a tragic end for Greeley, who in the space of little more than one month had lost his wife, his election, a substantial amount of money, and his own life.

Unsung Coaches

Gerald Ford and Woodrow Wilson have a little-known achievement in common: Besides being presidents, both of them served as football coaches. Gerald Ford was a star football player during his undergraduate days at the University of Michigan. He then moved on to Yale for law school in 1935, where he served as an assistant coach of the varsity football team while attending law school off and on over the next five years.

And Woodrow Wilson? He helped out with the football team when he taught at Princeton, but was never listed as an official coach.

FAST FACT

There are lots of towns but only one state named for a president: Washington.

(Un)lucky Charm

President William McKinley always wore a scarlet carnation, the official flower of McKinley's home state of Ohio, in his lapel. He considered it a lucky charm.

On Sept. 6, 1901, President McKinley made a trip to Buffalo, New York, for a business exposition. A little girl in the crowd admired his carnation, so McKinley took it off and gave it to her. A kind gesture, but perhaps not a very smart one.

Later that day, when McKinley was in a receiving line at the exposition—without his lucky carnation—a man named Leon Czolgosz, who was known as an anarchist, came up to McKinley and fired two deadly shots at him.

McKinley thus became the third president to be assassinated in just thirty-six years, following Abraham Lincoln (in 1865) and James Garfield (in 1881). McKinley was buried in his hometown of Canton, Ohio, with a red carnation in his casket.

Jackson's Heroic, but Unnecessary, Battle

If news had only traveled faster, General Andrew Jackson might never have become a national hero. Jackson led American troops to victory over the British in the famous Battle of New Orleans in the War of 1812—but in a curious twist, it turned out the battle was all for naught.

Fifteen days before the battle, England and America had signed a peace treaty in Europe, ending the war. But communication was so slow then that Jackson and the British troops had no idea the war was over, so they kept fighting. Luckily, Jackson won, and his fame in winning that battle led Congress to award him a special gold medal and gave politicians the idea to run him for public office. He was elected to the U.S. Senate from Tennessee, and later, to the presidency.

FAST FACT

Four state capital cities honor presidents: Jackson, Mississippi; Jefferson City, Missouri; Lincoln, Nebraska; and Madison, Wisconsin.

He Should Have Known Better!

William Henry Harrison was the only president who had studied to become a medical doctor. He went to the University of Pennsylvania medical school at the urging of his father, who wanted William, more than anything else, to be a doctor.

But when Harrison's father died, Harrison dropped out partway through medical school and did what he really wanted to do. He became an officer in the army.

Harrison had a long military career until he entered politics, running for the U.S. House of Representatives from Ohio. Later he became a U.S. senator and then president.

Ironically, Harrison, the only president with medical training, didn't take very good care of himself. At his inauguration ceremonies, at age sixty-eight, on a blustery, wintry day, he insisted on giving a long speech outdoors without a hat or coat. He caught pneumonia, and died just thirty-one days later. Of all people, he should have known better!

Presidents King and Blythe

Have you heard of Presidents Leslie King and Bill Blythe? It's not surprising that you haven't, but they were indeed presidents of the United States. Confused yet?

Those were the birth names of Gerald Ford and Bill Clinton.

Leslie King's mother and father divorced soon after Leslie was born. Mrs. King then married a man named Gerald Ford, who adopted little Leslie and gave him the name of Gerald Ford Jr.

Bill Clinton's parents were William and Virginia Blythe. His father died and his mother later remarried, to a man named Roger Clinton. At age sixteen, the future president changed his name from Bill Blythe to Bill Clinton. Make sense now?

The Teetering Veep

On March 4, 1865, Andrew Johnson was inaugurated vice president under President Abraham Lincoln—the man he would soon succeed as president. But Johnson's behavior that day was pretty un-vice-presidential.

You see, Johnson had been suffering from typhoid fever and doctored himself by drinking too much whiskey. At the inauguration ceremony, he walked with the aid of the outgoing vice president, Hannibal Hamlin. Johnson was unsteady and his face was flushed. He then gave a disjointed speech that embarrassed those in attendance.

Luckily for Johnson, it was a kinder and gentler time in this nation's history: He was forgiven when it became known that he had been ill and was generally not a drinking man.

> *Lucy Hayes, the eighteenth first lady, was the first to have graduated from college.*
>
> **FAST FACT**

All in the Family

Benjamin Harrison's first wife, Caroline, became ill and was an invalid during the last years of Harrison's presidency. Her niece, Mary, came to live in the White House to help care for her, but Caroline Harrison died six months before the end of her husband's term. Romance blossomed for the widower: After leaving the White House, Benjamin Harrison married the niece, who was twenty-four years his junior. They had a child when Harrison was sixty-four years old.

FAST FACT

POPULAR, BUT NOT PRESIDENTIAL
No one with the most common last name in America, Smith, has become president.

Old Man Eloquent

John Quincy Adams was known as "Old Man Eloquent." It wasn't just that he was a great speaker, he was a great speaker in *seven* languages!

As a young boy, Adams attended schools in France, Holland, and Russia when his father moved from one diplomatic assignment to another. Then he went to college at Harvard, where he studied classic languages.

By the time he was a young adult, Adams could speak French, German, Dutch, Greek, Latin, and Russian . . . and, of course, English.

A Sad Day for Roosevelt

Theodore Roosevelt's wife *and* mother both died—

of completely unrelated causes—on the same day in the same year.

Roosevelt's wife, Alice, died in childbirth, and his mother, Martha, died of typhoid fever, both in New York City. The date was February 14, 1884—ironically, Valentine's Day.

And what of the baby? She was named Alice, after her mother, and grew up to be a famous Washington hostess and outspoken critic of presidents for many years.

Everybody Was LBJ

Do you know what a lady bird looks like? The Taylor family cook must have, because she thought the two-year-old Claudia Alta Taylor was "pretty as a lady bird." A nickname was born: For the rest of her life, little Claudia was known as Lady Bird.

When she married Lyndon Baines Johnson, they both shared the initials LBJ—but that was only the beginning. They named their two daughters Lynda Bird Johnson and Luci Baines Johnson. And even their dog got into the act: He was named Little Beagle Johnson.

FAST FACT

Only three chief executives were referred to often by their initials: FDR (Franklin Delano Roosevelt), JFK (John Fitzgerald Kennedy), and LBJ (Lyndon Baines Johnson).

The Power of Fashion

President Theodore Roosevelt threw a spectacular White House wedding in 1906 for his daughter Alice and Congressman Nicholas Longworth. The press covered the wedding extensively, and doted on the shade of Alice's untraditional but beautiful blue wedding gown. The shade became known as "Alice blue."

Soon after, two leading songwriters of the day, Harry Tierney and Joseph McCarthy, wrote a hit song that swept the nation and has become a standard. The song, called "Alice Blue Gown," was later featured in the Broadway show *Irene*. Too bad the show wasn't called *Alice*!

George Washington's Achilles Heel

Despite Washington's popularity and successes, some historians say he suffered a major inferiority complex—not because of his wooden teeth, but because of his lack of education.

Washington had little formal schooling and never attended college. Most of his colleagues in government, however, were highly educated men. His vice president, John Adams, was a Harvard man. Thomas Jefferson was a graduate of William & Mary College and later a founder of the University of Virginia. Alexander Hamilton had gone to Columbia. And James Madison was a Princetonian.

Washington reportedly often felt ill at ease with these men and regretted his limited education. It didn't seem to hold him back though, did it?

> George Washington died in the last hour of the last day of the week, in the last month of the year, in the last year of the 1700s.
>
> **FAST FACT**

The Unhappiest President

Many presidents had rough times during their terms, but for consistent troubles and personal grief, nobody beats Franklin Pierce.

Before Pierce even took office, two of his three children had died, one in infancy and another at age four. And then, less than two months before he assumed the presidency, Pierce's third child, a twelve-year-old son, was killed in a railroad accident.

Pierce's wife, Jane, was understandably grief-stricken and had no enthusiasm to serve as first lady. She did not attend her husband's inauguration and the traditional Inaugural Ball was canceled. She dressed in black throughout her husband's term and remained in seclusion for much of the time.

But it wasn't just Pierce's family that was plagued. Just one month after Pierce took office, his vice president, William King, died. And as if that wasn't enough, Pierce had to deal with the increasing bitterness between the North and South that was leading up to the Civil War. He was also blamed for the 1857 financial panic that hit the nation.

To round out Pierce's unhappy time, he failed to get his party's nomination for a second term. Perhaps it was just as well....

Though people today are generally bigger than those who came before, Abraham Lincoln still holds the record for being the tallest president at six feet four inches.

FAST FACT

"What's This Country Coming To?"

In 1964, a movie star who had tap-danced and acted in more than thirty musical films and light romances—George Murphy—was elected United States senator from California. He was the first Hollywood actor to achieve a high national political office.

The thought of an actor entering the hallowed halls of the U.S. Senate shocked some Americans, and comments like, "What's this country coming to?" were not uncommon. One jokester in Hollywood reportedly said at the time, "The next thing you know, they'll be running Ronald Reagan for president."

Well, sixteen years later, they did.

Not So Fast, Arnie

The 2003 election of Arnold Schwarzenegger as governor of California recalls the same path that Reagan took. Reagan was governor of California before becoming president—but there's a major difference. Under the Constitution as it now reads, Schwarzenegger is ineligible for the presidency because he was not born in the U.S.; only a Constitutional amendment could make him eligible. Don't worry: He'll be *baaack*.

The Shortest Presidential Term

Did you know we once had a president that served only twenty-four hours? Well, we did, and not because of some horrible tragedy. It was all because of the day of the week. Zachary Taylor was supposed to be sworn in as president on March 4, 1849—but March 4 fell on a Sunday that year, and Taylor refused to take the oath of office on a Sunday.

The outgoing president and vice president's terms ended constitutionally at noon that day, so the U.S. would be without a president for twenty-four hours, or until noon on March 5. Next in line was the president pro tempore of the Senate, David Atchison. Some historians claim that Atchison was technically the U.S. president for those twenty-four hours.

If something had happened that day that would have required presidential action, Atchison would have been the person to perform it. Fortunately, nothing of significance took place and Atchison spent the day, as he later said, sleeping and writing letters.

But that didn't stop Atchison's home state of Missouri from erecting a monument to him on his death thirty-seven years later. The inscription on it reads: "David Rice Atchison . . . President of U.S. one day."

Campaign Slogans Miss the Mark

Sadly, presidential candidates often make promises they find hard to keep after they've been elected. But few have ever been as far off target as Herbert Hoover.

When Hoover ran for president in 1928, he campaigned on the optimistic slogan: "A chicken in every pot; a car in every garage," forecasting great prosperity for America. Hoover got elected, but boy, did his slogan ever miss the mark. Less than a year after he took office, the stock market crashed, the Great Depression followed, and many Americans went hungry; breadlines were common, and buying a car was completely out of the question for a substantial number of people.

Despite the less than favorable odds, Hoover didn't give up. When he ran for reelection in 1932, his slogan was "Prosperity is just around the corner." Hoover lost his bid for reelection, and the Depression continued to deepen. Maybe Hoover should've hired new writers!

You Win Some, You Lose Some

Imagine losing a mayoral race only to become president later. Theodore Roosevelt was the only person to run for mayor and lose, but then later run for president and win.

Amazingly, this future popular president couldn't get enough votes to win a mayoral election in New York City in 1886.

Why did Roosevelt lose his mayoral bid? Part of the blame may be due to the fact that he had been out of the city for two years, spending his time on his North Dakota ranch. He returned to New York to run for mayor, but with a late start in the race, lost badly.

The presidential election of 1904 was a different story altogether. By that time Roosevelt was a national hero following his command of the Rough Riders in the Spanish-American War. He had been elected vice president in 1900 under William McKinley and had served as president upon McKinley's assassination in 1901.

When he ran for president on his own in 1904, he won easily, beating his main opponent, Alton Parker, by more than two million votes. It's a good thing Teddy didn't give up!

> Three men who had been mayors of their cities eventually became president: Andrew Johnson, Grover Cleveland, and Calvin Coolidge.
>
> **FAST FACT**

The Irony of Nixon's Big Win

In 1972, Richard Nixon scored a historic victory: He became the first man to win forty-nine states in a presidential election.

Running against George McGovern, Nixon carried every one of the fifty states except Massachusetts. Nixon even won McGovern's home state of South Dakota.

The irony is that despite that historic win, Nixon could not complete his term. Two years into it, he was overwhelmed by the Watergate scandal and resigned from office.

A further irony is that the Watergate break-in was made to gather information on his opponents to help Nixon's campaign—help he wouldn't have even needed, considering the easy victory he scored in the election.

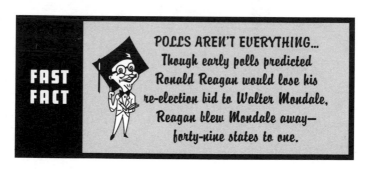

FAST FACT

POLLS AREN'T EVERYTHING...
Though early polls predicted Ronald Reagan would lose his re-election bid to Walter Mondale, Reagan blew Mondale away— forty-nine states to one.

First Sons

Aside from the two presidential sons who became presidents themselves—John Quincy Adams and

George W. Bush—five other sons of presidents tried to get nominated for the job.

They were: Charles Adams, son of John Quincy; John Van Buren, son of Martin; John Harrison, son of William Henry; Robert Lincoln, son of Abraham; and Robert Taft, son of William Howard.

None made it.

Thirteen Years Without a President?

Did you know the U.S. once went thirteen years without a president? Sounds crazy, but it's true!

The country was formed in 1776, but George Washington did not take office as the first president until 1789. Yet, during those thirteen years, the U.S. got off the ground, won the Revolutionary War, and functioned as a successful, independent nation—all without a president.

How was the nation run? The government was operated by the Continental Congress. Although there was no president, the congress was populated by such leaders as Benjamin Franklin, Thomas Jefferson, George Washington, Patrick Henry, Alexander Hamilton, John Hancock, and John Adams. They and other delegates from the thirteen states governed the country on a daily basis while debating and compromising on states' rights versus federal rights in drafting a permanent constitution and creating a new republic.

Finally in 1789 the U.S. Constitution was adopted, and America had its first president. But all in all, while waiting for a chief executive, the congress didn't do a bad job.

Jimmy Madison and Jimmy Monroe?

Presidents James Madison and James Monroe were never called Jimmy by the press or when introduced for a speech—and in fact, no president ever insisted on being referred to by his nickname until James Earl Carter came along in 1977. He let it be known that he wanted to be called Jimmy Carter.

Other presidents had nicknames, like Theodore "Teddy" Roosevelt or Dwight "Ike" Eisenhower, but those names were not used in any kind of formal setting. The only other president besides Carter who continually went by his nickname was Bill Clinton.

You Can't Always Get What You Want

Harold Stassen, a bright, charismatic man, was elected governor of Minnesota at age thirty-one in 1939. He was called The Boy Wonder—and many politicians and others predicted he would someday become president of the United States.

Well, Stassen was reelected governor twice, but it was all downhill from there. He tried for the presidential nomination nine times, but failed each time. After he moved to Pennsylvania, he also tried for nominations for governor there, and for mayor of Philadelphia, but failed to get those, too.

Stassen became something of a laughingstock in his futile quest. It was a sad journey for a man who was considered a brilliant thinker. In his lifetime he had been a lawyer, educator, advisor to presidents, decorated World War II hero, and a force in the founding of the United Nations. But he could never get the job he wanted most: president of the United States.

Love and Marriage

The first divorced man ever to become president was the fortieth president, Ronald Reagan, elected in 1980. Reagan had been married to the Academy Award–winning movie star Jane Wyman. They divorced shortly after Wyman won her Best Actress Oscar for *Johnny Belinda* in 1948. Reagan then married another movie actress, future first lady Nancy Davis.

Five other presidents were married twice, in each case marrying after their first wife's death. Those presidents were John Tyler, Millard Fillmore, Benjamin Harrison, Theodore Roosevelt, and Woodrow Wilson.

Members of the White House staff told an uncharacteristic story about Wilson. Wilson's first wife, Ellen, had died early in his first term, in 1914. Wilson married Edith Bolling Galt, the widow of a Washington jeweler, a year later. On the night of his wedding, Wilson introduced her to the staff—and the usually austere, dignified Wilson broke out in song, serenading her with "Oh, You Beautiful Doll." Love is a many splendored thing, or so they say.

Happy Days?

The Democrats chose "Happy Days Are Here Again" as their theme song when Franklin Roosevelt was campaigning for his first presidential term in 1932. The song is still played at Democratic conventions today, even though it has a slightly strange history.

"Happy Days Are Here Again" was first published on October 29, 1929, the very day the stock market crashed, ushering in the Great Depression. And when the song was used in the '32 campaign, days were anything but happy, as America was still deep in the Depression.

And perhaps the most ironic thing about the Democrats' favorite song? It was written by Jack Yellen, a staunch lifetime Republican.

Presidential Stepping Stone

A surprisingly high number of U.S. presidents—twelve of the first forty-two—have been generals in the army.

Here they are, with the wars they fought in:

George Washington in the Revolutionary War.

Andrew Jackson in the War of 1812.

Zachary Taylor in the War of 1812, the Indian Wars, and the Mexican War.

William Henry Harrison in the Indian wars.

Franklin Pierce in the Mexican War.

Andrew Johnson, Ulysses Grant, Rutherford Hayes, James Garfield, Chester Arthur, and Benjamin Harrison in the Civil War.

Dwight Eisenhower in World War II.

No admiral has ever made it. There was some talk of running Admiral George Dewey for president after his victory at Manila Bay in the Spanish-American War, but it never happened.

Eerie Coincidences

The assassinations of Abraham Lincoln and John Kennedy had an incredible number of eerie coincidences surrounding them:

Both men were shot on a Friday.

Both were seated beside their wives when shot.

Neither Mrs. Lincoln nor Mrs. Kennedy was injured.

Lincoln was in Box 7 at Ford's Theatre. Kennedy was in car 7 in his motorcade.

The assassins both went by three-word names—each with fifteen letters—John Wilkes Booth and Lee Harvey Oswald.

Lincoln was elected president in 1860, Kennedy in 1960.

Both their last names have seven letters.

Each of their successors was named Johnson—Andrew Johnson and Lyndon Johnson, and both of those names contain thirteen letters. Andrew was born in 1808, Lyndon in 1908.

Oswald shot Kennedy from a warehouse and hid in a theater. Booth shot Lincoln in a theater and hid in a warehouse.

Booth and Oswald were each killed by a single shot from a Colt revolver before they could be brought to trial.

Both Lincoln and Kennedy were pronounced dead in a place that had the initials PH—Lincoln in the Peterson House and Kennedy at Parkland Hospital.

Lincoln had sons named Robert and Edward. Kennedy had brothers named Robert and Edward.

And the final coincidence: The car in which Kennedy was riding when he was shot was . . . a Lincoln.

VP by Day, Barkeep by Night

Richard Johnson, VP under President Martin Van Buren in 1837, didn't think his $5,000 salary was enough. So to supplement his income, he opened and ran a tavern in Washington—all while serving as the nation's vice president.

Interestingly enough, no one really seemed to mind. The media didn't pay much attention to it, and Johnson was popular on Capitol Hill, having served in both the House and Senate from Kentucky before becoming vice president. Besides, most taverns were respectable places, also serving as inns in those days.

VP Johnson had been awarded a ceremonial sword by Congress for outstanding bravery during the War of 1812. This accolade made him a hero to many people, plus he hung the sword in the bar, which no doubt helped business!

Fireside Chats Were Hot . . . but Not Really

When Franklin Roosevelt became president in 1933, he found a new way to communicate with the public. Network radio had begun just a few years earlier, and Roosevelt was the first president to take advantage of it on a regular basis. Going on the air often, he made informal reports to the American people while seated by a fireplace in the White House. CBS news reporter Bob Trout, who often introduced the president, coined the name for Roosevelt's chats. He called them "Fireside Chats," and they became a famous feature of Roosevelt's presidency.

The significance of the Fireside Chats was enormous. Roosevelt harnessed the new power of radio to enter living rooms across the nation with his inspirational talks during the tough times of depression and war. Political experts say the effectiveness of the Fireside Chats was a major factor in Roosevelt's reelection successes.

The weird thing is that unbeknownst to many, the actual fireplace where Roosevelt broadcast his chats was the only one in the White House that didn't work. It's a good thing that TVs weren't common yet!

It All Could Have Been Hers . . .

When George Washington was twenty, he proposed marriage twice to a sixteen-year-old girl, Betsy Fauntleroy, but she turned him down both times. Little did this daughter of a Virginia planter know in 1752 of the greatness that lay ahead for her suitor.

Washington was crushed and wrote that he received a "cruel blow." Six years later, he married a rich widow, Martha Dandridge Custis. She was a year older than Washington and reputed to be one of the richest women in Virginia. Her first husband had been the

wealthy landowner Daniel Custis. From all indica-
tions, George and Martha had a happy marriage, but
Martha didn't enjoy being first lady. She once even
wrote that she felt like a "state prisoner."

George and Martha were married for forty years.
She died three years after her husband and was
buried beside him at Mt. Vernon. And what, you
might ask, became of Betsy Fauntleroy? She could
have been the *first* first lady, but instead her name
is all but lost to history.

This Election Amazingly Ends in a Tie

The presidential election of 1800 ended in an exact
dead heat, marking the only time in history that two
presidential candidates received the same number
of votes in the Electoral College. Thomas Jefferson
and Aaron Burr set the record when they both got
seventy-three electoral votes. A new record's always
nice, but the country needed just one new president.

Under the rules at the time, it was up to the House
of Representatives to decide. Thirty-six ballots were
taken, and finally the House made Jefferson the president. The House then made Burr the vice president,

even though Jefferson and Burr were rivals who had just run against each other.

That may seem shocking, but because the original Constitution was written without regard to political parties, the candidate with the second most electoral votes became VP. It soon became obvious that a change was necessary so that presidents and vice presidents could run as a team with clear-cut candidates for each position. The Twelfth Amendment to the Constitution was quickly rushed into effect to straighten that out before the next election. (If the Twelfth Amendment had never been passed, George W. Bush, with the most electoral votes, would have won the presidency in 2000—and Al Gore, with the second most, would have been Bush's vice president. Now wouldn't that have been interesting?)

Hanging Sheriff Becomes President

The only county sheriff ever to become U.S. president was Grover Cleveland. He was sheriff of Erie County, New York, from 1870 until 1873, and was elected president eleven years after leaving his sheriff's post.

But his position as sheriff was notable as well. Cleveland was known as "The Hanging Sheriff" because contrary to custom, he had hanged two men himself. Most sheriffs delegated the actual hanging of convicted criminals to their deputies, but Cleveland did the deed himself, stating that he would not ask anyone else to do what he was unwilling to do.

Before becoming a sheriff, this future president worked as a clerk in a law firm for four dollars a week plus room and board. Then he served in a district attorney's office and ran successfully for sheriff. Following his hanging-sheriff days, Cleveland moved up the political ladder: He was elected mayor of Buffalo, New York; then governor of New York; and ultimately president of the United States.

First Families

It's pretty amazing that ten of the first forty-two men who served as president had a blood relationship to another president. John and John Quincy Adams and George H. W. and George W. Bush were father and son; William and Benjamin Harrison were grandfather and grandson; James Madison and Zachary Taylor were second cousins; and Theodore and Franklin Roosevelt were fifth cousins.

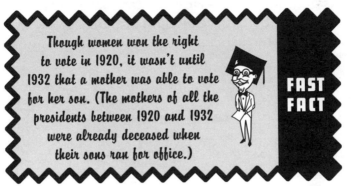

Though women won the right to vote in 1920, it wasn't until 1932 that a mother was able to vote for her son. (The mothers of all the presidents between 1920 and 1932 were already deceased when their sons ran for office.)

FAST FACT

From One White House To Another

How did George Washington get married in the White House in 1758 if it wasn't completed until 1800? Washington married Martha Custis at the bride's plantation home in New Kent County, Virginia, which, oddly enough, was called "The White House." Custis's mansion was named long before the presidential lodging was built in Washington D.C.

What Do You Do After You're President?

Aside from William Howard Taft, who became a Supreme Court justice after his presidency, only two other ex-presidents moved on to another regular high-level government job.

Two years after leaving the White House, John Quincy Adams ran for the U.S. House of Representatives from Massachusetts, and won a seat in Congress. He was subsequently elected to eight more two-year terms. Andrew Johnson ran for the U.S. Senate from Tennessee five years after his presidency, was elected, and served until his death during his first term.

Then there was Grover Cleveland. He had the most unusual post-presidential job of all. He became president again. Cleveland had served one four-year term from 1885 to 1889, but was defeated for reelection by Benjamin Harrison. He sat out four years as an ex-president, then ran again against Harrison and won a new four-year term from 1893 to 1897. Cleveland is the only man to experience the pomp and power of the highest office in the land, leave it, and then get it back again.

VP Indicted for Murder

Did you know that one of the U.S. vice presidents was indicted for murder?

Well, it's true. Aaron Burr, VP under Thomas Jefferson, was indicted for the 1804 killing of Alexander Hamilton in a duel. Burr left New Jersey, where the duel was fought, and completed his term as vice president in 1805.

He never returned to New Jersey and was never brought to trial on that indictment—though his legal troubles were far from over. In 1807 Burr was arrested and charged with treason for allegedly attempting to form his own republic in the American Southwest. He was put on trial, with Supreme Court Chief Justice John Marshall presiding. Because of conflicting testimony, Burr was acquitted, and he spent the remainder of his career as a lawyer in New York City.

The Money Man

The man killed by Vice President Aaron Burr, Alexander Hamilton, had been in the cabinet of the first

U.S. president. He was Washington's secretary of the Treasury and was considered a financial expert. In fact, he is credited with establishing sound money practices for the new nation.

Hamilton is honored today as one of the few non-presidents pictured on U.S. paper money. You can see his face on the ten-dollar bill. But what about Hamilton's own money situation?

When Aaron Burr's one pistol shot ended Hamilton's life, he was broke. He had managed his personal financial affairs so badly that he died heavily in debt. The man on the ten-dollar bill left no money for his wife and seven young children, and they had to be cared for by others.

Commander in Chief

Although all presidents are known as commanders in chief of the armed forces, and many have had some military experience, only one has actually ever led troops in battle while in office: James Madison. When the British invaded the area around the nation's capital in the War of 1812, President Madison left the White House and took command of those fighting to protect Bladensburg, Maryland. Madison even faced enemy gunfire. Ironically, Madison was one of the few presidents who had had no previous military training.

How Old Were Those Old-looking Presidents?

When you look at pictures of all the old presidents—with their distinguished brows and powder-white hair—don't they all seem to have been way past the senior citizen mark? Well, oddly enough, for 171 years—from George Washington in 1789 until Dwight Eisenhower's second term in 1960— no U.S. president had reached his seventieth birthday. All presidents up to Eisenhower were in their sixties or younger.

In fact, the U.S. has had only two seventy-plus-year-old presidents. Besides Eisenhower, who left office at age seventy, there was Ronald Reagan, who was inaugurated at sixty-nine and finished his second term at seventy-seven (making him the oldest president by far).

And what about Franklin Roosevelt, who was president for twelve years? He was only sixty-three when he died in office during his fourth term.

Presidential Longevity

Until 2001, John Adams held the record of being the longest-living president. In an era when few people lived to ninety years of age, Adams was 90 years, 247 days old when he died in 1826.

He held that record until October 11, 2001, when Ronald Reagan reached the age of 90 years, 248 days.

Only one other president lived to ninety. Herbert Hoover died at age 90 years, 71 days.

Something's Funny
About That Family Tree

Benjamin Harrison had a very average family—a wife, two kids, four grandchildren. Well, two years after his wife Caroline died, Harrison married a woman named Mary Dimmick. When Harrison was sixty-five years old, he and Mary had a baby daughter. Upon the baby girl's birth, the infant became aunt to nieces and nephews who ranged in age from one to eight years old.

And if that weren't confusing enough, Harrison's first two children were older than their new step-mother. When Harrison married Ms. Dimmick, his first child, Russell, was forty-two, and his second child, Mary, was thirty-eight. Ms. Dimmick was just thirty-seven at the time of her wedding to Harrison.

After leaving the presidency, Harrison moved to Indianapolis, where he practiced law and tried to keep his family straight. The public generally congratulated Harrison for fathering a child so late in life, and he wrote a book about government, called *This Country of Ours*, that was well received.

A President of the People

The first six presidents—Washington, Adams, Jefferson, Madison, Monroe, and J.Q. Adams—were all from relatively wealthy families and were members of the upper-class establishment. But the seventh president, Andrew Jackson, was the son of poor Scottish-Irish immigrants and was born in a log cabin. (Contrary to popular opinion, Abraham Lincoln wasn't the first president to have been born in a log cabin.)

Each of the first six presidents was from either Virginia or Massachusetts, but Jackson grew up in the then-frontier life of the Western Carolinas and Eastern Tennessee. Jackson earned the nickname

"Old Hickory" during a rough patch in his child-hood. He was said to be tough as hickory wood and got his first taste of war when he was only thir-teen, joining the militia to fight the British during the Revolutionary War.

This first president from humble beginnings grew up to be a respected army general, governor, U.S. senator, and as he called himself, a president of the people.

FAST FACT

Six Jameses have served as president—Madison, Monroe, Polk, Buchanan, Garfield, and Carter.

OK for President!

Did you know that one of the most often used words in the English language and many foreign languages was coined as a description for an American president?

Martin Van Buren, the man who ran for president in 1837, was from the little upstate New York town of Old Kinderhook. His supporters formed the "OK

Club" from the initials of his hometown, and they nicknamed him "OK." OK became the campaign slogan, and saying that Van Buren was OK meant that he was "all right" and "good." Over time, OK entered everyday language and was alternately spelled "okay." Either way, it meant that anyone or anything was all right.

Just think: If Van Buren had been from some other town, we probably wouldn't be using the word OK today. And things just would not be okay without it!

Call Him Mr. President OR Mr. Chief Justice

William Howard Taft was the only man to serve as president of the United States and chief justice of the U.S. Supreme Court. After leaving the presidency in 1913, Taft taught law at Yale for eight years, and then was appointed chief justice in 1921 by President Harding. He served on the court until illness forced him to resign in 1930. He died one month later.

Taft often said he enjoyed the Supreme Court more than the presidency. Maybe it was the robe?

First Female President?

In 1919, with seventeen months to go in his second term, President Woodrow Wilson suffered a devastating stroke that paralyzed the left side of his body. Unfortunately he became an invalid. But he did not give up his presidency.

The Constitution then did not address the problem of a president who becomes severely ill but does not die or resign. Since Wilson was bedridden for much of those seventeen months, his wife, Edith, often shielded him from cabinet members, congressional leaders, and the vice president. When there was a bill or an official letter to sign, Edith held Wilson's hand and guided it. She decided what messages got through to the president, and in some cases, according to various historians, made decisions about the affairs of the nation when she felt he was unable to do so.

So although she was not president in name, Edith Wilson did, at times, act as president.

Guess Who I Am

I failed in business.
I ran for state legislature, and lost.

I ran for the U.S. Senate, and lost.
I ran for the U.S. Senate again, and lost.
I ran for U.S. vice president, and lost.
I ran for U.S. president, and won.
My name: Abraham Lincoln.

The first president to be born in a hospital was Jimmy Carter; all others before him were born at home.

FAST FACT

The Pugilist

Harry Truman was known as a down-to-earth guy who usually didn't pull any punches, figuratively speaking. But he once threatened to really clock somebody—while he was president.

Truman doted on his daughter, Margaret, who aspired to be a singer. She gave a concert in Washington and was ferociously panned by *Washington Post* critic Paul Hume. Hume wrote, in part, "Margaret Truman is flat a good deal of the time . . . cannot sing with anything approaching professional finish . . . communicates almost nothing of the music."

The next day President Truman wrote the critic this acerbic note in response: "I have just read your lousy review . . . I never met you, but if I do you'll need a new nose and a supporter below."

Suffice it to say, Hume steered clear of 1600 Pennsylvania Avenue.

The Highs and Lows of Aaron Burr

Aaron Burr was a brilliant, successful lawyer and a hero in the Revolutionary War, honored for distinguished valor in the Battle of Monmouth. He became attorney general for the state of New York and was elected to the U.S. Senate and then the U.S. vice presidency at age forty-four.

A promising future seemed in store for Burr—but then it all came crashing down. After years of a bitter rivalry with Alexander Hamilton in their law practices and in politics, Burr challenged Hamilton to a duel. When Burr fatally wounded Hamilton with one shot and was indicted for murder, his political career was ruined. (Burr was never brought to trial on the charge, however.)

Many felt he shouldn't have been allowed to finish the remaining eight months of his term as vice president, and although he did, he would never run for office again.

This man who came so close to being president in his Electoral College tie vote with Thomas Jefferson quickly became one of the most unpopular men in America.

Ballpark First

At a baseball game in 1910, President William Howard Taft may have made history. For some reason, Taft had to leave during the game's seventh inning. The crowd, out of respect, stood as he exited the ballpark. According to some historians, this marked the beginning of the beloved baseball custom of the seventh-inning stretch.

While there's some dispute about that, there's no question that Taft did initiate another tradition. While in office he attended an opening day game and threw out the first pitch. From then on, every baseball season is begun with the president or another official throwing out the ceremonial first pitch.

The Terrible "Zero Jinx"

For 120 years, EVERY president elected in a year ending in zero died in office.

The jinx started with William Henry Harrison in 1840. Then came Abraham Lincoln, elected in 1860, James Garfield in 1880, William McKinley in 1900, Warren Harding in 1920, Franklin Roosevelt in 1940, and John Kennedy in 1960. All died in office. (The way elections work out, with one every four years, there were no presidential elections in 1850, 1870, 1890, 1910, 1930, or 1950.)

After John Kennedy, the next president elected in a zero year was Ronald Reagan in 1980. He broke the jinx—but just barely. An assassination attempt was made on Reagan by John Hinckley Jr. as he was walking out of the Hilton Hotel in Washington. Although a bullet entered Reagan's chest, he survived and finished his two terms.

FAST FACT

THE MAGIC OF FIFTY-SEVEN...
Four of the first six presidents were all the same age—fifty-seven—when they were inaugurated. None since has been.

Presidential Bloopers

Over the years the presidents have said some ringing lines that inspired the nation—and some that, well, weren't so hot. In the latter category was Richard Nixon's comment when he visited China's Great Wall in 1972. Reporters asked Nixon what he thought of the breathtaking monument. As they eagerly awaited a noteworthy quote, Nixon replied, "Well, I must say the Great Wall is . . . a great wall."

Then there was Calvin Coolidge's not-so-profound assessment of the economy. He said, "When more and more people are thrown out of work, unemployment results." Insightful, indeed!

And Gerald Ford undoubtedly lost votes when, during a campaign speech, he said, "Poland is not under Soviet domination." Unfortunately for Ford (and the Polish), it was.

Words from the Wise

Fortunately, not all presidential quips are inane and, worse, embarrassing. Some presidential words have been profound, illuminating, and even moving.

John Kennedy made history at his inauguration in 1961 when he said, "Ask not what your country can do for you; ask what you can do for your country." According to Kennedy historian Arthur Schlesinger, Kennedy had written variations of that famous quote in a loose-leaf notebook when he was twenty-eight years old. The idea for the quote came from Oliver Wendell Holmes, who had written in 1884, "Recall what our country has done for us, and ask ourselves what we can do for our country in return," and from a speech by Russell Briggs in 1904, when he said, "The youth who loves his alma mater will always ask, not what can she do for me, but what I can do for her."

When Franklin Roosevelt took office at the depth of the Great Depression, his aim was to rally the nation and pull it out of its despair. At his inauguration, he famously said, "The only thing we have to fear is . . . fear itself." Roosevelt set the tone, and nickname, for his first administration when, at his nomination acceptance speech, he said, "I pledge you, I pledge myself, to a 'New Deal' for the American people."

Then there were Abraham Lincoln's closing words in his Gettysburg Address, historic words about the preservation and future of the nation following the Civil War: "This . . . government of the people, by the people, for the people, shall not perish from the earth."

Now, That's a Lot of Cake

Poor George Washington. For a long time no one seemed to get his birthday right.

George was born on February 11, 1731—but when he was twenty-one years old, the calendar was changed. February 11 (Old Style) became February 22 (New Style) and so for the rest of his life, February 22 was his birthday.

Seem strange? The old calendar, developed by astronomers in 46 B.C. at the direction of Julius Caesar (and called the Julian calendar), was erroneous and had to be changed. It proved to be off by about eleven minutes each year based on the movement of the sun. (That doesn't sound like much, but the result was that gradually the seasons were being skewed so that they began at the wrong time.) Pope Gregory XIII had his astronomers make changes in 1582 to correct the calendar. They came up with the Gregorian calendar, which is still used today. The Catholic countries of Europe adopted the Gregorian calendar almost immediately, but Protestant countries like England and its colonies, including America, didn't make the switch until 1752. In order to convert from the Julian to the Gregorian, ten days were dropped from September 1752. (So a person going to bed on September 2, say at 11 P.M. and sleeping eight hours, would wake up at 7 A.M. to find it was September 13, not September 3.)

Dropping those ten days from a year moved everybody's birthday, including Washington's. This meant that from then on, Washington's birthday was celebrated on February 22 instead of on the 11th.

Depending on how you look at it, things got even more confusing in 1971. That year President Nixon signed an executive order on federal holidays that placed Washington's birthday on the third Monday in February. The date changes every year.

Bowdoin's Famous Class of 1825

Three of the twenty-four students in the 1825 graduating class of this small Brunswick, Maine, school went on to national fame.

Franklin Pierce became U.S. president. And two of Pierce's classmates (and fellow Phi Beta Kappa brothers) became famous authors. They were Nathaniel Hawthorne and Henry Wadsworth Longfellow.

Hawthorne became a major American novelist with his popular masterpieces such as *The Scarlet*

Letter and *The House of the Seven Gables*. He also wrote a book called *Fanshawe* that was set at a college similar to Bowdoin. And Longfellow turned out to be one of the nation's most beloved poets with his verses "Paul Revere's Ride," "The Song of Hiawatha," and "The Children's Hour," among others. He also wrote two of the most famous lines in American poetry: "Listen my children and you shall hear, of the midnight ride of Paul Revere."

Above and Beyond

In February of 1848 former president John Quincy Adams was giving a speech in the House of Representatives when suddenly he fell unconscious to the floor. Adams was arguing vehemently against a proposed bill that would give honorary swords to generals who fought in what Adams considered a "most unrighteous war" with Mexico.

House members and spectators gasped as, all of a sudden, Adams clutched his neck and collapsed. He had suffered a cerebral stroke. Too ill to be moved from the building, former President Adams was carried to the Speaker's Room at the rear of the chamber, where he died two days later.

Perhaps it was fitting that Adams's final days were on the job. After serving for four years as president, he did not take a rest from public service, but instead worked as a congressman for nearly sixteen years. At his funeral, Senator Thomas Hart Benton, the main eulogist, appropriately noted, "Where would death have found him except at the place of duty?"

Flash in the Pan

James Garfield had one of the shortest presidencies in U.S. history. On July 2, 1881, just a few months after his March 4 inauguration, Garfield set out to leave Washington to attend the twenty-fifth reunion of his class at Williams College in Massachusetts.

At the Baltimore and Potomac Railroad station preparing to board a train, Garfield was suddenly struck down by two pistol shots.

Garfield fell, and the suspect was immediately surrounded and arrested. Considering Garfield had been in office for such a short time, it's hard to imagine he'd have any enemies. So why did the assassin, Charles Guiteau, do it? Described as a disappointed office seeker, Guiteau had wanted to be appointed U.S. consul to Paris but didn't get the job. Guess he wanted it badly enough to kill for it. Guiteau pleaded insanity at his trial, but he was convicted of murder and hanged in 1882.

And what of Garfield? One of the shots grazed his arm, but the other bullet lodged in his body and doctors couldn't find it. They even called in Alexander Graham Bell, the inventor of the telephone, who had developed an electrical device they thought might help. Sadly, the bullet was never found and Garfield died of blood poisoning eighty days later on September 19, 1881, at age forty-nine.

Garfield had been president for just 199 days. The only president who had a shorter term was William Henry Harrison, who died of pneumonia thirty-one days after his inauguration in 1841.

The Very Wary Veep

Vice President Harry Truman got an urgent message on the afternoon of April 12, 1945: He was to report to the White House immediately. He was met there by Mrs. Eleanor Roosevelt. "Harry," she said, "the president is dead." Truman was floored. He later told reporters, "I felt like the moon, the stars, and all the planets had fallen on me."

Here was a man who was not even supposed to be vice president, suddenly thrust into the job of succeeding one of the strongest, most popular, most charismatic presidents ever, all while World War II raged on.

Truman, in contrast to Roosevelt, seemed to many then as a small, confused, totally out-of-place person. He had not been a major figure on the national scene before becoming vice president and did not appear to have the bigger-than-life presence of Roosevelt. Nevertheless, Truman rose to the occasion.

A Crash Course

Harry Truman had a lot of catching up to do when he assumed the presidency upon Franklin Roosevelt's death. As vice president, he had not been given intimate knowledge of the U.S.'s war and foreign policies—that was just the norm at the time. Neither Roosevelt nor anyone else had briefed him on national or international issues. He had to quickly come to grips with running the country.

As it turned out, of course, Truman did grow in the job, overseeing victory in the European phase of World War II, authorizing the dropping of the atom bomb on Japan, negotiating triumph over the Japanese to end the Pacific war, and leading America in the new post-war world. Many historians give Truman high marks for his work at a critical time—a far cry from the man who was so overwhelmed when he became president. Way to go, Harry. You sure showed 'em.

The Unlikely Heir

When President Franklin Roosevelt was preparing to run for a fourth term in 1944, insiders knew he was not in good health and unlikely to live another four years. Therefore, the selection of vice president was crucial.

The incumbent vice president Henry Wallace, Supreme Court Justice William Douglas, and former justice James Byrnes were the leading contenders for the job. Few political pundits ever mentioned Senator Harry Truman. However, on the eve of the Democratic Convention, Roosevelt surprised almost everyone by choosing Truman. Wallace later said that the president had told him that afternoon that he, Wallace, would be the VP. "What made him change his mind between 3:00 P.M. and midnight, I'll never know," Wallace said.

So what happened? Nobody knows for sure, but some historians say that at the eleventh hour Robert Hannegan, chairman of the party's convention, urged Roosevelt to take Truman as the VP choice. It was reported later that some powerful party leaders had grown wary of Wallace because of what were said to be his increasingly socialist ideas. Among the other candidates, Byrnes was considered by some to be too conservative and Douglas didn't have campaign experience. Apparently, Truman emerged as the last-minute alternative because influential party leaders liked his voting record in the Senate. The choice surprised the nation, and less than a year later, Truman would be president.

Ike and the Interstates

Did you know the U.S. interstate highways have an official name? You're not alone if you didn't. The official name is the Dwight D. Eisenhower Interstate System because it was President Eisenhower who proposed building the interstates after World War II.

His main motivation? To have good through-highways for rapid troop and truck deployments in the event of a future war.

If you're one of those people who struggles with maps, here's an easy guide to the interstates: Those that go basically east–west have even numbers, while north–south highways have odd numbers. The lowest-numbered interstates are in the south and west. All interstates are marked with red, white, and blue shield-shaped signs.

The total length of the interstate highway system is over 45,000 miles. Building them was the biggest public works project ever completed by the U.S. After Eisenhower proposed the interstates, Congress authorized them and building began in 1956.

Hindsight is 20/20

Daniel Webster was a long-time, powerful U.S. senator in the 1800s. Many thought he would be a U.S.

president someday, and Webster himself wanted the job.

Webster came close in 1840 when William Henry Harrison, who had just become a presidential candidate, offered the vice presidency to him, but Webster turned it down. Harrison was elected president, but died just thirty-one days after taking office. If he had only accepted Harrison's offer, Webster would have been president.

Webster's second chance came in 1848 when Zachary Taylor offered him the vice presidency. But again, Webster said no. He wanted to be president, after all, not vice president.

As bad luck would have it, Taylor died just a little more than a year into his term, and Webster lost his second chance to be president. He never did make it. Guess it just wasn't meant to be.

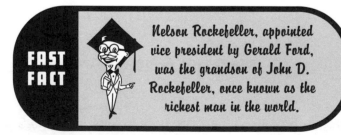

FAST FACT

Nelson Rockefeller, appointed vice president by Gerald Ford, was the grandson of John D. Rockefeller, once known as the richest man in the world.

Almost a No-Show

You know the old saying, "Location, location, location"? Well, real estate isn't everything. Just ask George Washington. He owned his Mt. Vernon estate in Virginia and other properties, but often found himself cash-poor.

In order to be inaugurated as first U.S. president, Washington had to travel to New York City, which was then the nation's capital, for the ceremonies. There was one major problem, though: He didn't have enough cash for the trip, and the government wasn't going to pay for it.

What was an almost-president to do? Washington turned to his friend and neighbor Richard Conway of Alexandria, Virginia. Washington wrote Conway a poignant letter in which he practically begged for money—not only for the trip, but also for other debts he owed. From the tone of Washington's letter, he was embarrassed, saying, in part, "This is so disagreeable to me. I am inclined to do what I never expected to be driven to do, that is, to borrow money on interest."

Washington blamed his money woes on "poor crops and other causes not entirely in my control." Washington asked for $500, but Conway went even further and loaned him $600. Thanks to Conway, the United States was able to inaugurate its first president.

FAST FACT

Both John Kennedy and Herbert Hoover donated their presidential salaries to charity.

The Cigar Aficionado

Many presidents have enjoyed cigars, but none smoked them like Ulysses Grant: He was reported to smoke about twenty a day. When word got out about his love of cigars, people sent thousands his way. Grant's response? "What was I to do? I gave some away, but I smoked the rest." No need, after all, to look a gift horse in the mouth!

Fact or Fiction?

Rumor has it that before President John Kennedy placed an embargo on all imports from Cuba, including cigars, he sent his press secretary Pierre Salinger to buy up all the Cuban cigars in the Washington area so that Kennedy would have his own supply.

When Salinger got back to the White House, Kennedy asked him if the buying trip was successful. According to the legend, Salinger said yes, and then Kennedy announced the Cuban embargo.

Ain't No Stopping Him

One of the most bizarre campaign speeches of all time was delivered by Theodore Roosevelt. In 1912 Roosevelt was running for president on a third-party ticket after having completed two terms as president four years earlier. He was speaking in Milwaukee on October 14, 1912, when a saloonkeeper, John Schrank, fired a shot at him. Schrank later said he was opposed to Roosevelt's try for a third term, and at his trial, was declared insane and committed to a mental institution.

The bullet went into Roosevelt's chest, but an eyeglass case in his coat pocket partially deflected the bullet—it probably also saved his life. Roosevelt was one tough cookie. He didn't let a bloodstained shirt or, worse, a bullet wound stop him. He insisted on completing his speech and spoke, incredibly, for fifty minutes while blood dripped down to his shoes.

When he was finally done, Roosevelt was rushed to a hospital. He survived, but lost the election.

An Old Familiar Tune

Did you know that we have the United Kingdom to thank for many of our most patriotic songs? James Sanderson of Scotland composed the stirring song "Hail to the Chief," played at public appearances of U.S. presidents. The words, which are seldom heard, were taken from the "Boat Song" in the famous poem "The Lady of the Lake," by another Scotsman, Sir Walter Scott.

Neither Sanderson nor Scott was ever in America, and had no idea their song would be used for U.S. presidents. We can thank John Tyler's wife, Julia, for that. In the early 1840s, Julia suggested the band play "Hail to the Chief" when President Tyler was to make an appearance at a public function, and the tradition was born.

The music of the "The Star-Spangled Banner" and "America" ("My Country 'Tis of Thee") also came from abroad. Francis Scott Key wrote the words for

"The Star-Spangled Banner," but the tune was taken from an old British drinking song, "To Anacreon in Heaven." The Rev. Samuel Smith wrote the words for "America" for a children's picnic in 1831 at his Park Street Church in Boston, but borrowed the tune directly from the British national anthem.

So How Does That Song Go Again?

Since few people know the words to the stirring "Hail to the Chief," played for U.S. presidents, we thought we'd give you a look.

Here they are as penned by Sir Walter Scott as tributes to a chief of Scottish tribes in his "Lady of the Lake":

Hail to the Chief of our beloved nation
Hail to the Chief in whom we put our trust
Hail to the Chief, our hope and inspiration
Serving the cause to preserve our liberty

With sincere devotion we support our commander
Knowing in him we can place our belief
May God always guide him and lead him on his way
Hail to the president, Hail to the Chief.

Kid's Camp

Did you ever wonder how Camp David, the famous retreat, got its name? The presidential playground in the Maryland mountains was originally built for President Roosevelt during World War II. He named it Shangri-La.

But when Dwight Eisenhower became president in 1953, he gave the official oasis a new name—something a bit more personal. He renamed it Camp David, after his young grandson David Eisenhower. And that's how it's been known ever since.

Talk About Multitasking

James Garfield found himself in a peculiar situation in November of 1880. Garfield was a member of the U.S. House of Representatives when the Ohio legislature elected him to serve in the U.S. Senate for a term starting the following March. But he was also running for president . . . and won that election.

Garfield was a member of the House, senator-elect, and president-elect—all at the same time.

You can probably guess which job he took. Not surprisingly, he resigned his House and Senate seats and set off for Pennsylvania Avenue.

The Lobby That Started It All

While president from 1869 to 1877, Ulysses Grant made a habit of relaxing most evenings at the Willard Hotel, which was near the White House. Grant would sit in the lobby of the hotel and enjoy an after-dinner cigar (one of the twenty he was reputed to smoke each day). Those seeking favors from the president found this to be an ideal opportunity. They waited for him in the lobby, and not so creatively, earned the name "lobbyists."

And that, dear readers, is how the word came into our language to describe those seeking to influence politicians.

Pocahontas's Legacy

The first Native American to live in the White House

was Edith Wilson, the wife of President Woodrow Wilson. She was a direct descendent of the famous American Indian Pocahontas. Pocahontas earned legendary status in the early 1600s, when she saved the life of Captain John Smith, the leader of English settlers near Jamestown, Virginia.

Smith had been captured by the Indian chief, Powhatan, during a battle between the two groups. Smith was condemned to death and Powhatan was about to kill him when Powhatan's twelve-year-old daughter, Pocahontas, stepped in front of Smith and begged her father to relent. Smith later wrote of the incident and Pocahontas became a hero among the American settlers and the British back home.

A few years later, Pocahontas married Englishman John Rolfe. Their descendents became members of prominent families in Virginia.

Charles Curtis Makes History

For the first 140 years of the U.S. presidency, not one descendent of a Native American served as either president or vice president.

All that changed in 1929, when Charles Curtis, whose mother was a full-blooded member of the

Kaw Indian Tribe of Kansas and Oklahoma, was elected VP under President Herbert Hoover.

Curtis was a long-time member of Congress and had been Senate majority leader before serving as VP with President Hoover. He was a popular politician who spoke proudly of his Native American heritage.

The President Who Changed Football

Teddy Roosevelt did more than just inspire the production of cuddly stuffed bears—he also played a pivotal role in making football what it is today. In the early days of American football, starting in 1869 with the first intercollegiate game, passing wasn't allowed.

You see, football evolved from British soccer, where only goaltenders are allowed to touch the ball. Gradually, American football rules were changed to allow running with the ball, and then finally in the late 1800s, the forward pass was legalized. Few teams, however, took advantage of it. Instead, they slugged it out at the line of scrimmage, resulting in an alarming number of injuries and even deaths.

Americans were horrified by the violence of the game—so much so that there were cries to abolish it altogether. President Theodore Roosevelt stepped onto the scene in 1904 and convened a meeting of coaches and officials at the White House. He ordered them to put in more passing, open up the game, and decrease the injuries. Thanks to Roosevelt, football was saved and arguably made more wide-open, appealing, and safer!

"Lemonade Lucy"

There were a lot of rules at the White House when Rutherford Hayes was president from 1877 to 1881. Hayes's wife, Lucy, had a list of no-no's: no dancing, no smoking, no card playing, no drinking. Sounds like no fun.

But Mrs. Hayes, before becoming first lady, had been a leading campaigner in the country for prohibition of alcohol sales. She and her husband led a religious life, starting each day with a morning prayer service and gathering with friends to sing hymns on many evenings. So Mrs. Hayes stood by her beliefs. She would serve nothing stronger than lemonade at White House receptions, earning herself the nickname of "Lemonade Lucy." Instead of wine flowing like water, the country joked that water flowed like wine.

But that's not Lucy's only claim to fame. She is also remembered for starting the annual children's Easter egg roll on the White House lawn. The event had previously been held at the Capitol building, but Congress stopped it because some members complained it was damaging the grass on the Capitol lawn. Lucy gladly agreed to have it at the White House, where she gave the children Easter eggs and, of course, lemonade.

Size Isn't Everything

James Madison was the smallest president, standing a mere five feet four inches and weighing less than one hundred pounds while in office. But though Madison didn't weigh much, he was no mental lightweight. He was a giant among the Founding Fathers, responsible for drafting the first ten amendments to the Constitution, the Bill of Rights. For that and other contributions, he was called the "Father of the Constitution."

Madison's wife, Dolley, was somewhat taller and much heavier than her husband. Author Washington Irving once wrote, "Mrs. Madison is a fine, portly, buxom dame. As to Jeemy Madison—ah! poor Jeemy!—he is but a withered little apple-John."

And what about the other end of the presidential scale? William Howard Taft weighs in as our heaviest president: He stood six feet tall and weighed more than 300 pounds.

Post-presidential Woes

Ulysses Grant had about $100,000, mostly saved from his annual presidential salary of $50,000, when he finished his eight-year presidency in 1877. Grant left the White House and returned to Galena, Illinois, where he had lived before becoming a general in the Civil War. Sadly, hard times were in store.

Grant invested all his money in the banking company Grant & Ward, which was run by his son, Ulysses Jr., and a partner. But unfortunately the company failed and Grant lost his entire investment. The former president was practically penniless. (Back then there was no such thing as a presidential pension.)

To make ends meet, Grant began writing magazine articles about the Civil War, and then wrote an autobiography called *Memoirs*. He did not live to see the fruit of his labors. Grant died, still broke, before the book was published. But *Memoirs* became a big best seller and his family eventually earned royalties totaling more than $500,000.

Earning It the Easy Way

Here's an easy way to win a bet. Ask someone to name the presidents pictured on all the U.S.'s currently circulated paper money—the $1, $2, $5, $10, $20, $50, and $100 bills. You'll be surprised at how few people can do it, even though we handle money every day.

The first thing to remember is that two of those bills don't have presidents. The $10 bill has the first secretary of the Treasury, Alexander Hamilton, and the $100 bill features Founding Father Benjamin Franklin. Neither was ever president.

So what about the rest? Go ahead and see if you can do it—and no peeking!

The $1 bill has George Washington; the $2 bill, Thomas Jefferson; the $5 bill, Abraham Lincoln; the $20 bill, Andrew Jackson; and the $50 bill, Ulysses Grant. Commit that to memory and you might find yourself making easy cash next time you're out at a bar!

Quick Change

It's not unusual to have two presidents in one year (think about when administrations switch), but what about three? And though it seems strange, it happened not once, but twice, in American history.

The first time was in 1841. Martin Van Buren completed his term on March 3 and was succeeded by William Henry Harrison. But Harrison died on April 4, leaving Vice President John Tyler to become president. So in the span of just thirty-two days, the U.S. had three presidents.

The second time was in 1881. James Garfield took over when Rutherford Hayes left office on March 3. But Garfield died in September that year, and VP Chester Arthur became president.

No Respect

When John Adams was vice president, he described it as "the most insignificant office that ever the invention of man contrived or his imagination conceived."

Daniel Webster felt similarly about the position. He refused an offer to run for vice president by saying, "I do not propose to be buried until I am really dead and in my coffin."

But it was John Nance Garner, Franklin Roosevelt's first vice president, who put it in the most colorful terms. He said the vice president's job "wasn't worth a pitcher of warm spit."

No Simple Feat

Many vice presidents have tried to be elected to succeed the president they served under, but only four have actually done it. John Adams succeeded George Washington in 1796, Thomas Jefferson succeeded Adams 1800, and Martin Van Buren succeeded Andrew Jackson in 1836. And then nothing for 152 years until Vice President George Bush succeeded Ronald Reagan.

As for failures, the most recent was Al Gore in 2000.

The Gray-Brown House

The White House wasn't always white. It was originally

built of sandstone and was grayish-brown in color. Not surprisingly, it wasn't called the White House back then. Instead, it was called the President's House or Executive Mansion.

But all that changed during the War of 1812 when the invading British army burned parts of the building's exterior. The house was painted white after the war to cover up the burn marks. Gradually, people began calling the president's home the White House, and the name was made official when Theodore Roosevelt became president in the early 1900s.

Presidential Laundry

The White House wasn't completed until late in the term of the second U.S. president, John Adams. In 1800 when Adams and his wife moved in, the house still wasn't finished.

Understandably, Mrs. Adams was not happy with her living conditions. She complained that her family had use of only six rooms and the main stairs weren't in place. And, because the grounds were still clogged with construction equipment, she had to hang her wash in the East Room. Now that must have been a sight.

Short and
Not So Sweet

Parting is such sweet sorrow . . . especially when it's just after you've said hello. When William Henry Harrison was inaugurated as the ninth U.S. president on March 4, 1841, he didn't realize his first speech might be his last.

The stubborn sixty-eight-year-old man caught a cold after he refused to wear a hat or coat on that frigid, wintry day. He spent an hour and forty-five minutes delivering his 8,578-word inaugural address, the longest on record, and then led a parade to the White House.

Unfortunately, Harrison's cold turned into pneumonia in the days following. Instead of heading off to the Oval Office, Harrison was ordered to bed. Important business was turned over to aides and members of Congress, and Harrison, by then severely debilitated, was only able to approve a few minor appointments.

After spending most of his term in bed, Harrison died just thirty-one days after his inauguration, on April 4, 1841. Besides giving that record-breaking speech, Harrison never did anything significant as president. If only he hadn't been so stubborn, he might have at least signed a bill. . . .

A Swimming Streak

John Quincy Adams loved to sneak out of the White House and swim nude in the Potomac River. This was well known at the time, and Adams swam on more than one afternoon.

One day, a crafty female reporter who had been trying to get an interview with Adams went to the banks of the Potomac and snatched his clothing. She threatened to keep them unless he agreed to give her the interview. Adams relented, got out of the water, and put his clothes back on while she discreetly turned away.

You'd think Adams would have learned his lesson, but he refused to surrender his splashy hobby, and could still be found skinny-dipping on the days he could get away from the White House. Just imagine if the tabloids of today had been around then!

Cup o' Joe

The Maxwell House in Nashville, Tennessee, is a well-known old Southern hotel that served a special blend of coffee. When President Theodore Roosevelt visited there, his hosts asked him if he'd like another cup of coffee. Teddy famously replied, "Yes. It's good to the last drop." When Maxwell House coffee was later marketed to the world, Roosevelt's words were immortalized as their slogan.

Everyone's got to be a critic, though. Over the years, some wags have asked, "What's wrong with the last drop?"

The Buzz on Facial Fuzz–
Part 1

It's been a long time since we've had a mustached president in office. The last one was William Howard Taft, who served as president from 1909 to 1913. Thomas Dewey, who wore a mustache, almost made the presidency in 1948, but was upset by the clean-shaven Harry Truman.

The Buzz on Facial Fuzz–
Part 2

Five presidents wore beards in office—all in the late 1800s.

Abraham Lincoln was the first, followed by Ulysses Grant, Rutherford Hayes, James Garfield, and Benjamin Harrison. Since Harrison left office in 1893, no president has worn a beard.

Perhaps it's just a coincidence, but all the bearded presidents were Republicans.

Letting Bygones Be Bygones

Andrew Johnson was the only president to be elected to the U.S. Senate after leaving the presidency.

Johnson served as president from 1865 to 1869, then was elected a senator from Tennessee in 1874. But when Johnson entered the Senate, he was taking his seat among many men who had voted on his impeachment when he was president. He was seated with the very same men who had found him "guilty of high crimes and misdemeanors."

(During his impeachment trial, thirty-five senators voted him guilty and nineteen not guilty. Since a two-thirds vote is necessary for conviction, Johnson was acquitted by the margin of one vote.)

Despite the strained atmosphere anticipated when Johnson first entered the chambers as a senator, there was a surprising result. He was warmly greeted with applause, flowers were sent to his desk, and during his tenure neither he nor his colleagues mentioned much about the impeachment.

You've Come a Long Way, Baby

When future president Andrew Johnson was sixteen years old in 1824 he still could not read or write. He never made it to school, instead spending much of his childhood working.

But when he was seventeen, his girlfriend Eliza McCardle taught him to read and write. Johnson married her when he was nineteen, later making her the first lady of the land.

Despite his lack of formal education, Johnson held political office at virtually every level of government. He was mayor of Greeneville, Tennessee, a member of the state legislature, governor of Tennessee, a U.S. congressman, and vice president and president of the United States.

Now That's a Party!

When Andrew Jackson was inaugurated in 1829 as the seventh U.S. president, he threw open the White

House doors and invited all his old buddies to stop in. What a mistake that was.

Jackson came from humble beginnings, unlike the first six presidents, who were all descended from aristocratic families. Jackson considered himself a man of the ordinary people, and many of his former neighbors and friends were rough frontiersmen. They attended his inauguration ceremonies, and he sent word that they should all come to the White House that evening for a party.

The party turned out to be a drunken brawl: Visitors broke glasses, stood on chairs with muddy boots, destroyed furniture, yanked down wall hangings, and fought. It got so bad that Jackson had to escape through a rear window and spent his first night as president in a hotel above a tavern. Cleanup of the White House was begun the next day.

Chances are Jackson's friends weren't invited back.

Forget Something?

If you were to sum up Thomas Jefferson's life, what would you say? Well, near the end of his life, Thomas Jefferson did just that and wrote the epitaph for his grave.

Jefferson wrote that he authored the Declaration of Independence, the statute for religious freedom in Virginia, and had been the father of the University of Virginia.

Strangely, he neglected to mention one of the things for which he was most well known: He left out the fact that he had been president of the United States. Think it just slipped his mind?

The Red, not White, House

Many plans were considered for the building of the president's home in the late 1700s. Thomas Jefferson, who among his many accomplishments was an architect, suggested a house of red brick, similar to homes he knew in his beloved Virginia. But the commission that made the final decision chose James Hoban to design the presidential home, and Hoban's design did not call for red brick.

But what if Jefferson's idea had prevailed? The leaders of the Cold War's two main adversaries, the Soviet Union and America, would have been based respectively in Moscow's Red Square and Washington's Red House. And anti-Red statements would have been issued from the Red House. It sure would have made things confusing.

FAST FACT

Three graduates of U.S. military academies have gone on to become president: Ulysses Grant, Dwight Eisenhower, and Jimmy Carter.

World War II Vets

Seven of the eight men who were president during the forty years from Dwight Eisenhower through George H. W. Bush served in the armed forces during World War II. Can you guess which one of the eight didn't?

Eisenhower, John Kennedy, Lyndon Johnson, Richard Nixon, Gerald Ford, Ronald Reagan, and Bush all saw service in World War II.

The lone exception in that string of eight consecutive presidents was Jimmy Carter, who later served in the navy but missed World War II. The young Carter couldn't serve because he was still at the naval academy when the war ended.

Oops!

When future president Andrew Jackson was twenty-four years old, he married Mrs. Rachel Robards (née Donelson). Little did he know that his marriage would spark a controversy.

Mrs. Robards believed she had obtained a divorce from her first husband, an army captain named Lewis Robards, when she married Jackson in 1791. But it turned out the divorce wasn't final. Still, Jackson and Mrs. Robards continued to live together as Mr. and Mrs. Jackson. They had another marriage ceremony three years later when the official divorce decree finally came through.

Not surprisingly, Jackson's political opponents dogged him on the issue the rest of his career and some even accused him and his wife of adultery. But the accidental bigamy didn't harm Jackson's political career. In fact, he easily won the presidential election of 1828 over John Quincy Adams with sixty-eight percent of the electoral vote. Four years later he won a second term by an even bigger margin, seventy-seven percent over Henry Clay.

Ivy League Alums

The eight colleges known as the Ivy League have produced more than one-fourth of all U.S. presidents.

Harvard men included John Adams, John Quincy Adams, Theodore Roosevelt, Franklin Roosevelt, and John Kennedy, plus George W. Bush, who earned a master's degree from Harvard Business School.

James Madison and Woodrow Wilson went to Princeton.

William Henry Harrison attended medical school at the University of Pennsylvania.

Yale grads were William Howard Taft, George H.W. Bush, and George W. Bush, plus Gerald Ford and Bill Clinton, who both received degrees from Yale Law School.

But what about the other four schools—Brown, Columbia, Cornell, and Dartmouth? Though none of them produced a future president, Columbia appointed Dwight Eisenhower as its president four years before he became leader of the U.S.

FAST FACT

Harry Truman is the only twentieth- or twenty-first-century president who never went to college.

"Tippecanoe and Tyler Too"– and Other Campaign Slogans

Did you know that "Tippecanoe and Tyler Too" was the first successful, memorable slogan used in a presidential election campaign? Do you know what it means? Captain William Henry Harrison achieved fame by leading his troops to victory in a famous battle against Tecumseh's forces during the Indian wars in 1811. The battle was held in the little town of Tippecanoe, Indiana, located on the Tippecanoe River. When Harrison ran for president in 1840 with John Tyler as his running mate, the catchy slogan "Tippecanoe and Tyler Too" was coined and helped Harrison win the election.

Since then, of course, there have been many famous campaign slogans: James Polk's "Fifty-four Forty or Fight" (referring to a border latitude dispute with England); Abraham Lincoln's "Don't Swap Horses in the

Middle of the Stream," for his second term during the Civil War; William Howard Taft's "Get on the Raft with Taft"; Woodrow Wilson's second term slogan, "He Kept Us Out of War" (which Wilson did in his first term, but not in his second); Warren Harding's "Return to Normalcy"; Calvin Coolidge's "Keep Cool with Coolidge"; Franklin Roosevelt's "New Deal"; Harry Truman's use of the song "I'm Just Wild About Harry"; Dwight Eisenhower's "I Like Ike"; Lyndon Johnson's "All the Way with LBJ"; and Richard Nixon's "Nixon's the One."

The Anti-slogans

As we all know, the race for the presidency can often get ugly. Many colorful, not-so-nice slogans have been created about presidents over the years, including some of the following zingers: Senator Robert Taft's line about Harry Truman, "To Err is Truman"; Lyndon Johnson's assessment of Gerald Ford, "He played too much football with his helmet off"; the Republican campaign's slogan against Franklin Roosevelt and his wife, Eleanor, "We don't want Eleanor either." And there were more. Rutherford Hayes was referred to by his opponents as "His Fraudulency" because of his disputed election. Grover Cleveland was called the "Beast of Buffalo" for the hangings he conducted when he was a sheriff in Buffalo, New York.

And the pro–Richard Nixon campaign slogan, "Nixon's the One," was turned against him after he claimed that he had nothing to do with the Watergate break-in scandal.

Three Out of Five On the Fourth

In a bizarre coincidence, three of the first five presidents all died of unrelated causes on the anniversary of the nation's Independence.

John Adams, the second president, died on July 4, 1826. Thomas Jefferson, the third president, died on that very same day, July 4, 1826. And, James Monroe, the fifth president died on July 4, 1831.

Close, but no Cigar

The curious oddity of three of the first five presidents all dying on July 4—amazingly—came close to being four out of five.

James Madison, the fourth president, died on June 28, 1836—missing the July 4 date by just six days.

Of the first five presidents, only George Washington escaped the seemingly odd curse of July 4. He died on Dec. 14, 1799.

Don't Mess with Texas

George W. Bush fashions himself a Texan. And though Bush served as governor of Texas before becoming president in 2001, Texas is really just his adopted home.

Dubya, a member of the prominent Bush family of New England, was born in New Haven, Connecticut, on July 6, 1946. His grandfather, Prescott Bush, was a wealthy investment banker and a U.S. Senator from Connecticut from 1952 to 1962. And like his father, George H. W. Bush, George W. attended the prestigious New England prep school Phillips Academy in Andover, Massachusetts.

Then he followed family tradition by entering Yale University in New Haven, Connecticut, where, again like his father, he was a member of the elite, secret

Skull and Bones Society that has only fifteen members at any one time.

It was only after earning a master's degree from Harvard Business School that George W. left the Northeast for good and traded in his ties to New England for a Texan twang. He began his adult career in business and politics in Texas and eventually bought a ranch in Crawford, Texas. And it was there that this ex-Northeasterner adopted his Texas-style boots, belt buckles, and hats.

President Thomas Wilson?

Ask someone if Thomas Wilson was ever a U.S. president and you might just win a bet. Though no U.S. president ever went by that name, Thomas Wilson was indeed a president.

Thomas Woodrow Wilson was in fact the real name of the twenty-eighth president.

The name Thomas came from his maternal grandfather and the name Woodrow was his mother's maiden name. As a child, he was called by his first name, "Tommy," but he stopped using the name

Thomas soon after graduating from college. Upon entering the academic world as a professor, Wilson felt that Woodrow sounded more dignified. The name stuck, and little Tommy was known as Woodrow for the rest of his life.

So Close, and Yet . . .

When presidential election returns came in on the night of Nov. 7, 1916, it looked like Charles Evans Hughes was the winner over Woodrow Wilson.

Many people went to bed thinking Hughes would be the next U.S. president. Hughes himself went to bed at 1:00 A.M., convinced he had won. The election wasn't over, though. Late returns came in that changed the outcome, and the election actually went to Wilson.

A reporter called Hughes's room to get his reaction. A Hughes aide who answered the phone said, "The president is asleep." The reporter said, "When the president wakes up, tell him he's not the president." There's a reason they say *It ain't over 'til it's over*.

Vice Presidential Switch

In 1972, the Democrats had nominated George McGovern to run for president and Thomas Eagleton for vice president against Richard Nixon and Spiro Agnew.

But shortly after the campaign started, stories began circulating that Eagleton, a senator from Missouri, had been treated for depression earlier in his life. At first, McGovern said he would not replace Eagleton, but as the controversy grew, Eagleton agreed to step aside.

Sargent Shriver, the brother-in-law of former President John Kennedy, became the new candidate.

The switch didn't seem to make much difference. The Nixon-Agnew ticket beat McGovern and Shriver with a landslide win.

Pistols in the Senate?!

Back before he was president, Martin Van Buren presided over the Senate as vice president. It was under his watch that pistols were openly seen in the Senate for the first and only time.

Why? Van Buren supported a controversial bill that sparked rumors of a potential assassination.

The controversy centered on the power of the Bank of the United States versus state banks. Van Buren had long campaigned to give more power to state banks that he felt were closer to the people and therefore more likely to help farmers and local businesses. Opponents wanted a stronger national bank that they believed would insure safer money policies.

The dispute was so bitter that Van Buren began to fear for his life, especially when he was told that someone would be out to get him if he tried to break a Senate vote the "wrong way."

So Van Buren began carrying two loaded pistols wherever he went—and he often put them out on a table right in front of him in the Senate chamber.

All's well that end's well. Van Buren's opponents passed their bill, and nothing bad happened to the previously endangered VP. Van Buren lived another twenty-five years and died of natural causes at age seventy-nine.

One Heck of a Class

Hampden-Sydney College, a small school located in the southern Virginia town of the same name, boasts one of the most remarkable college classes of all time. The class of 1791 had just eight students, but one became a U.S. senator, one a U.S. congressman, one a state senator, one a state representative, one a college president, one a presidential cabinet member, and one a judge.

The eighth student in that class dropped out in his senior year, but even he went on to a fairly important job. His name was William Henry Harrison, and he went on to become president of the United States.

The Sky's Not the Limit

When the Constitution was adopted, there were no term limits for the president. Theoretically, the same person could be elected to the office any number of times.

George Washington, however, set a precedent of sorts during his second term by saying two terms were enough. In the years following, there was talk of running a two-term president for another term. Legally it was possible, but men such as Thomas Jefferson, James Monroe, and Andrew Jackson declined to try for a third term, citing Washington's precedent.

In fact, no president served more than eight years until the critical years of the Great Depression and World War II, when Franklin Roosevelt agreed to run for a third term.

He made history in 1940 with his third election, and four years later ran again and won a fourth term.

Roosevelt could have been president for at least 16 years had he not died early in his fourth term. As it was, he served twelve years and thirty-nine days.

The complicated Twenty-second Amendment, which prohibits any person from being elected president more than twice, was adopted shortly after Roosevelt's death. Though a president is limited to two terms under the amendment, he or she could actually serve a maximum of ten years. How? By completing two years or less of his or her predecessor's term, then being elected to two full four-year terms of his/her own.

A Long, Strange Trip

Gerald Ford is the only person in history to serve as vice president *and* president of the United States without ever being elected in a national election for either office. Seem unreal?

Well, when the elected vice president Spiro Agnew resigned in 1973, Ford was named VP to replace him under provisions of the Twenty-fifth Amendment to the Constitution. That amendment, ratified in 1967, says that any time there's a vacancy in the office of the vice president, "the president shall nominate a vice president who shall take office upon confirmation by a majority vote of both houses of Congress."

Ford easily won confirmation as VP. He had been a member of the House of Representatives from Michigan for over twenty-five years and had been the House minority leader.

As chance would have it, the president under whom Ford was serving, Richard Nixon, also resigned. And so, in 1974, Ford automatically became president. What a long, strange trip.

The Double Resignations

The Republicans had it rough in the early 1970s. Both the president (Richard Nixon) and vice president (Spiro Agnew)—serving together—resigned their offices for entirely different reasons.

Agnew, in his second term as VP in 1973, was suddenly accused of extortion, bribery, and income tax evasion as a result of investigations dating back to when he was governor of Maryland from 1967 to 1969.

His lawyers made a deal with a federal judge. The deal, to take effect on October 10, 1973, was this: Agnew would plead nolo contendere to one count of tax evasion, pay a $10,000 fine, be sentenced to three years probation, and resign as vice president in "the national interest."

Reports were that the administration was anxious for Agnew's resignation because President Nixon was facing the increasing possibility of impeachment over the Watergate break-in and his alleged cover-up of the crime. They wanted to remove Agnew from the line of succession to the presidency.

By the next summer, Nixon faced imminent impeachment. When he realized he no longer had a strong enough political base in Congress to avoid impeachment and possible conviction, Nixon resigned on August 9, 1974.

The Presidents Who Didn't Wear Pants

None of the first three U.S. presidents wore trousers or long pants. No, they did not share a common penchant for skirts. Instead, these men—George Washington, John Adams, and Thomas Jefferson—wore breeches or knickers, as did most upper-class men in the eastern part of the U.S.

The style began to change in the early 1800s, partially influenced by the French Revolution. The revolutionists wanted to make a statement against the breeches worn by the nobility and began dressing in long trousers like the common man. Because of this, the revolutionists were called the *sans-culottes*, which means "without breeches."

American leaders, in sympathy with the both the French Revolution and democratic ideals at home, began changing their style of dress. By the early 1800s, many fashionable men in the U.S. had discarded their breeches and were wearing long pants.

The first U.S. president to wear modern-type long pants on a regular basis was the fourth president, James Madison, who took office in 1809.

When You've Got to Go . . .

When the White House opened in 1800, it had no indoor plumbing. That meant that all the early presidents, including John Adams, Thomas Jefferson, James Madison, James Monroe, and John Quincy Adams, had to use outhouses on the White House grounds.

While that may sound sort of, um, unsavory to us, there was nothing unusual about people using outhouses into the 1830s and beyond. The modern bathroom as we know it today, with bathtubs and flush toilets, came relatively late to human civilization.

Even the magnificent palace at Versailles, which was built in the seventeenth century for the French royal family and had spectacular fountains and beautiful rooms, had no indoor plumbing for bathrooms or toilets.

And many homes in America, especially in rural areas, didn't get indoor plumbing until well into the 1900s. Even in cities, a lot of working-class homes didn't have indoor bathrooms until the late 1800s or later. The outhouse, often with a half-moon cutout on the door, was a famous symbol of everyday living for some up through World War II. So in some ways the White House was ahead of its time—it got indoor plumbing in 1833, when Andrew Jackson was president.

Thanks,
but No Thanks

According to all available evidence, James Polk hated being president.

He came to the presidency in 1845 after a twenty-year career as a U.S. congressman and governor of Tennessee—and apparently was tired of being a public servant. So how did the man who wrote that he longed to be a private citizen with "no one but myself to serve" end up as president? Polk was picked as a surprise, compromise candidate, and scored a big upset victory in the 1844 election.

Even though Polk was highly regarded and served at a time when things were going generally well for the nation, he wrote that he would "rejoice" when his term was over. Predictably, he put his money where his mouth was during his first term by absolutely refusing to run for a second term.

When Polk left office, he wrote, "I am sure I'll be happier in my retirement than I have been during the four years I have filled the highest office in the land." Unfortunately, he didn't really get the chance to find out: Polk died of a cholera attack at age fifty-three, only 103 days after leaving the White House.

The Funny Thing About Polk's Presidency

Although he didn't want the job and couldn't wait until his term was over, James Polk turned out to be—according to many historians—one of the most effective presidents in history. Polk was also one of the most underrated. He's usually not mentioned with the great presidents, but in Polk's one term the nation achieved many successes.

The U.S. won the Mexican War, forcing Mexico to give up all claims to Texas. But that's not all: Under the terms of the peace treaty, Polk's administration got control of all or part of present-day Arizona, California, Colorado, Nevada, New Mexico, Utah, and Wyoming.

And the long-simmering boundary dispute with England was finally settled by Polk's determined negotiations, giving the U.S. clear ownership of the present states of Idaho, Oregon, and Washington.

Polk also took good care of the economy, overseeing general prosperity and optimism in the nation in a time that became known as the fabulous forties.

Imagine what he could have done if he'd actually wanted to be president!

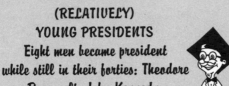

(RELATIVELY) YOUNG PRESIDENTS

Eight men became president while still in their forties: Theodore Roosevelt, John Kennedy, Bill Clinton, Ulysses Grant, Grover Cleveland, Franklin Pierce, James Polk, and James Garfield.

FAST FACT

You Snooze, You Lose

Charles Dawes, the vice president under Calvin Coolidge, was an accomplished man. He shared the 1925 Nobel Peace Prize with Sir Austen Chamberlain of England for arranging the plan for German reparations after World War I; he was the first director of the U.S. federal budget when that position was created in 1921; the U.S. ambassador to Great Britain; the first chairman of the Reconstruction Finance Corporation; and, finally, the chairman of the board of the City National

Bank of Chicago for nineteen years, until his death in 1951. With all that Vice President Charles Dawes did in his life, perhaps he could be excused for falling asleep on the job one time—but his little nap proved costly.

As VP, Dawes was presiding over the Senate in 1925 when a critical debate was taking place on whether to approve Charles Warren as attorney general of the United States. The Senate was fairly evenly divided on the issue. Under the Constitution, the vice president is the president of the Senate and the person who breaks a tie. So if the Senate was deadlocked when it came time to vote, Dawes would have to cast the deciding ballot.

The debate on Warren was under way. Dawes figured it would be long and drawn out, so he decided to go back to his hotel for a mid-afternoon nap and return in time for the vote. Alas, the Senate finished the debate sooner than expected and voted 40–40. A call was made to Dawes's hotel. Warren supporters tried to stall, knowing Dawes would vote for Warren. Dawes rushed back, but it was too late: One vote was switched while he was en route. Charles Warren lost 41–39, and never did become attorney general.

Silent, and Frugal, Cal

Ironically, while most of the country binged during the Jazz Age of the 1920s with new prosperity, wild stock market speculation, and carefree living, the man in the White House was shy, reclusive, frugal Calvin Coolidge.

Stories of Coolidge's frugality became legend. Once he gave a dime to an aide to have someone go out and buy a three-cent newspaper. When his change was not returned immediately, he reportedly made a big stink around the White House that someone owed him seven cents.

And when his son, Calvin Jr., took a laborer's job, one of Junior's fellow workers said, "If my father was president of the United States, I wouldn't be doing this kind of work." Junior replied, "If my father were your father, you would." And for a big White House reception, the kitchen staff ordered six hams, but Coolidge told them that five were quite enough.

While Coolidge was famous for his frugal ways, he did splurge on expensive cigars. Rumor has it that he would keep the expensive ones for himself and hand out the cheap five-cent cigars to friends and visitors. Some friend.

Honoring Thy Mother

If George Washington's mother had had her way, America would still be under British rule.

Mary Ball Washington did not want her son to join the revolution against England. She was perfectly content with things as they were, and she was not alone. Many Americans at that time who were of British ancestry had no desire to break away from England.

Even after the successful end to the revolution, Mrs. Washington still didn't change her mind. In fact, she was so against her son becoming president of the United States that she refused to attend his inauguration. Some historians say that Mrs. Washington didn't want George to become president because she wanted him to stay home and take care of her. Guess we'll never know. . . .

Father Figure

Even though George Washington is known as the father of our nation, he was never actually a father himself. Washington was twenty-six when he married the twenty-seven-year-old Martha Dandridge Custis. They were married for forty years and had no children. Martha had four children from a previous marriage, two of whom died in infancy, but George Washington never had any children of his own.

According to all reports, George was a loving and indulgent stepfather to Martha's two living children, John and Martha. Entries in the meticulous diaries he kept show that he bought them many toys and gifts and treated them as if they were his biological children.

Washington was one of six presidents who never fathered any children. The other five were James Madison, Andrew Jackson, James Polk, James Buchanan (the only president who never married), and Warren Harding.

The Only Foreign Capital Named for a President

In 1822, the American Colonization Society bought land in West Africa's Upper Guinea as a home for freed U.S. slaves. The newly created nation, called Liberia, honored America by naming its capital, Monrovia, after the president at the time, James Monroe. It was quite an honor, but ironically, Monroe was a slave owner at his home in Virginia.

Tit for Tat

The capital of one U.S. state is named for the head of another country. Can you guess the state and the capital? If you guessed Bismarck, North Dakota, you'd be right. Yet the capital of North Dakota wasn't always Bismarck. It was originally called Edwintown, and in 1873 was changed to Bismarck in honor of German president Otto von Bismarck.

Wondering what prompted the change? North Dakotans wanted to encourage German immigrants to settle there. What better way than by honoring the German head of state?!

A Loyal Employee

One of the fundamental positions held by the United States—that no foreign nation has the right to seize any part of North, Central, or South America—was put forth in the historic Monroe Doctrine.

It might come as a surprise, however, that although it's named after President James Monroe, who was president at the time the doctrine was announced—he neither wrote nor conceived it.

So whose idea was it? The idea came from John Quincy Adams, secretary of state under Monroe. Adams feared that some European countries might want to restore South and Central American colonies that had recently become independent, or that they might want to try to create new ones.

Adams wasn't off base. A few nations have tried to violate the doctrine since its proclamation in 1823, but all have failed. The U.S. successfully invoked the doctrine to settle the Oregon-Washington state boundary dispute with England in 1845, and it deterred France from intervening in Mexico in the 1860s.

So why isn't it called the Adams Doctrine? Adams drafted the language, but being a good underling, named it after his boss.

A Tough Fall for Ford

No, this wasn't another classic case of the clumsy Ford taking a fall. In the space of just seventeen days during the fall of 1975, Gerald Ford faced two separate, unrelated assassination attempts.

Miraculously, he escaped unharmed both times.

On Sept. 5, 1975, Ford was walking out of the Senator Hotel in Sacramento, California, where he had just given a speech, when a Charles Manson follower, Lynette "Squeaky" Fromme, aimed a pistol at him. Luckily a Secret Service agent grabbed the pistol before Fromme could fire it.

It was an odd thing that Fromme turned would-be assassin. No one who knew Squeaky as a kid would have expected violence from her. She was a former high school cheerleader from a middle-class Los Angeles family. But in her twenties Squeaky met and fell under the spell of cult leader Charles Manson. Manson convinced her and other followers that he was the Messiah and that his goal was to kill wealthy celebrities. After Manson was sent to prison for the murder of actress Sharon Tate, Fromme wanted to carry on his work and commit a famous crime. Instead, she was sentenced to life in prison for her failed assassination attempt. Squeaky's nickname, by the way, was coined from her high-pitched voice.

The Second Try on Ford's Life

Seventeen days after Squeaky Fromme tried to assassinate him, President Gerald Ford found himself in San Francisco, California. In an eerie repeat of the previous episode, Ford was coming out of a hotel—this time, the St. Francis—where he had spoken, when another woman, Sara Jane Moore, fired a pistol at him. Luckily for Ford, she missed.

Shockingly, Moore was a former employee of the FBI. She had been active in the counterculture movement in California and had been recruited by the FBI to gain inside information on the kidnapping of newspaper heiress Patty Hearst by a counterculture group.

After her friends found out she was working for the FBI, they turned against her. Wanting to reconnect with them, Moore decided to shoot the president of the United States to show her friends she was still with them.

Just as she was ready to fire at Ford, a bystander, Oliver Sipple, stepped in. He pushed her arm and caused the bullet to miss Ford. It ricocheted off a wall and wounded a cab driver (who survived). Like Fromme, Moore was sentenced to spend the rest of her days in prison.

Gerald Ford once said "I'm a Ford, not a Lincoln." Quite prophetic, when you consider his assassination-attempt survivals.

FAST FACT

Ouch

When Andrew Jackson was president, Harvard wanted to give him an honorary doctor's degree, an LL.D. Jackson, a popular president, had never gone to college.

In response, John Quincy Adams, Jackson's predecessor in office, wrote a scathing letter to the president of Harvard. It said, "As myself, an affectionate child of our alma mater, I would not be present to witness her disgrace in conferring her highest literary honors upon a barbarian who could not write a sentence of grammar and hardly could spell his own name."

Harvard gave the degree to Jackson anyway.

The Silly, Dishwatery Gettysburg Address

Abraham Lincoln's Gettysburg Address ranks as one of the most stirring and memorable speeches in history.

Yet after Lincoln made his speech, the *Chicago Times* gave this harsh review:

"The cheek of every American must tingle with shame as he reads the silly, flat and dishwatery utterances of a man who has to be pointed out to intelligent foreigners as the president of the United States."

As Lincoln might say, "You can't please all of the people all of the time."

The Empty White House

From 1948 through 1952, there was no president in the White House. It's not that the country didn't have a leader, but rather that the White House was beginning to show its age.

At that time the White House was 150 years old and there were fears that its structure had weakened, and improvements had to be made. Rather than have the president live and work through all the mess of a projected four-year renovation, reconstruction, and redecoration, it was decided to move him out of the house.

So President Harry Truman left, but he didn't go very far. The president, his staff, and family moved across the street to Blair House. Blair House is located on Pennsylvania Avenue and faces the north side of the White House. Blair House is a historic mansion, used for many years as an official guesthouse for top foreign visitors. It was built in 1824 and named after its owner, Francis Blair, an influential newspaper editor. The Blair family sold the house to the government in 1942, and it was from there that President Truman governed the nation for four years of his nearly eight-year term.

Non-resident President

President James Madison also had to leave the White House—for almost three years of his term in the 1800s. This time it was also because of renovations, but the renovations were necessary because of war.

On June 18, 1812, the U.S. declared war on England in what became known, logically, as the War of 1812. The war was caused by a dispute with the British over their blockading and seizing American ships. At the time, the British were at war with France and tried to prevent U.S. ships from supplying goods to the French and other European ports.

As the War of 1812 spread from the seas to land, the British invaded the U.S. They attacked and burned parts of the White House, causing President Madison to flee to Virginia for a short time.

When the siege of the nation's capital ended, he moved into the Octagon House in Washington while the White House was being repaired and painted. The Octagon House, just west of the White House at the corner of Pennsylvania Avenue and Nineteenth Street, was the private home of a friend of Madison, Colonel John Taylor. It must have been quite an honor for Taylor to have the country run from his home!

Record Holders

It's pretty funny when you think about it. The only man elected twice as vice president plus twice as president of the United States is the very same man who was forced to resign his office. Richard Nixon was elected VP two times, in 1952 and 1956. He was then elected president two times, in 1968 and 1972. No one else has accomplished that feat.

The only man to better that record was Franklin Roosevelt, who was elected president four times, in 1932, 1936, 1940, and 1944. But he never had the honor of being pressured to step down!

Now That's
a Snub

Can you imagine ignoring the death of a former president? It happened to John Tyler, who had been president from 1841 to 1845. Tyler died in 1862 in Richmond, Virginia.

The Civil War was raging at the time, and since Tyler lived in the South, President Lincoln took no official notice of Tyler's passing. There were no flags flown at half-staff, no government announcement, and no proclamation.

Tyler earned the dubious honor of being the only president whose death was officially disregarded.

An Affair
to Remember

When Grover Cleveland was campaigning for president in 1884, word leaked out that he had possibly fathered an illegitimate son. Cleveland, a bachelor at the time, said he wasn't sure he was the father, but he didn't deny it, either. Regardless, he agreed to support the boy.

A woman named Maria Halprin was the mother, and she added to the controversy by giving her son the middle name of Cleveland. The boy's name was Oscar Cleveland Halprin.

Supporters of Cleveland's opponent, James Blaine, had a field day with Cleveland's supposed indiscretion. They had a song written during the campaign that went, "Ma, Ma, where's my pa? Gone to the White House, Ha Ha Ha." But it didn't hurt Cleveland. In fact, he won the election.

Grover Cleveland's daughter Esther was the first and only child of a president to be born at the White House.

FAST FACT

A Fateful Meeting

Vice President Gerald Ford went to see President Richard Nixon on a routine matter during the afternoon of August 9, 1974. Suddenly Nixon turned to him and said, "You will do a good job in the presidency,

Jerry." And that's how Ford found out that Nixon was going to resign over the Watergate scandal. Nixon resigned that evening, and Ford became president.

In a controversial move less than a month after he assumed the presidency, Ford, who was not involved in the Watergate mess, pardoned Nixon for any federal crimes he may have committed. The pardon outraged many people. There were those who suspected a deal was made before Nixon resigned, but Ford always denied he had promised Nixon a pardon. Others wanted Nixon brought to trial to try to get to the bottom of the Watergate story.

So why did Ford issue the pardon? He said that "now our long national nightmare is over," and that the country could get on with its business.

As it turned out, the country got along without Ford two years later. Some said the pardon cost him the 1976 election when he ran for a second term.

Sibling Rivalry

Two brothers made history by once receiving electoral votes in the same presidential election. No other pair of siblings has matched them yet.

Brothers Charles and Thomas Pinckney of South Carolina both got electoral votes in 1796, but neither made it.

Instead, John Adams was elected president.

The Pinckney brothers both remained active in politics in the Federalist Party after that. Charles ran unsuccessfully for vice president in 1800 and for president in 1804 and 1808. Thomas later became governor of South Carolina and a U.S. congressman.

Meanwhile, their mother, Elizabeth, had a special bond to the presidency. She had inherited large plantation holdings in the South from her husband and had been a close friend of George and Martha Washington. When Elizabeth died in 1793 while Washington was president, he requested permission to be a pallbearer at her funeral and the request was granted.

Ike's Perfect Record

Most presidents were involved in political campaigns before they ever ran for president, but not Dwight Eisenhower. He ran for public office only twice in his life—in 1952 and 1956—and was elected president of the United States both times.

Eisenhower had led the Allied armies to victory in Europe during World War II, and both Democrats and Republicans wanted to run him for president in 1948. He refused by saying, "Lifelong professional soldiers should not enter politics." But by 1952, Republicans, with an "I Like Ike" campaign, finally convinced him to try for the presidency.

At the national convention, he was nominated on the first ballot and then easily won the election over his Democratic opponent, Adlai Stevenson. Four years later he scored an even bigger victory, running again against Stevenson, and then retired undefeated in political elections.

The Incredible Adlai E. Stevenson

Democratic President Grover Cleveland's vice president for his second term, from 1893 to 1897, was Adlai Ewing Stevenson.

Fast forward to 1952 and 1956, and the Democratic presidential candidate was Adlai Ewing Stevenson.

Confused? This is not some case of bizarre time travel: Adlai, the 1893–97 VP, was the grandfather of Adlai, the 1952–56 presidential candidate.

Foot-in-mouth Disease

Most U.S. vice presidents don't say much that's memorable during their stays in office.

The ill-fated Spiro Agnew was a major exception to that rule. While he was VP under Nixon, Agnew became famous (or infamous) for colorful alliterations denouncing the Vietnam War protesters. He called the protesters such attention-getting names as "nattering nabobs of negativism," and "hopeless, hysterical hypochondriacs." He also called them an "effete corps of impudent snobs."

Agnew also made a most unfortunate remark that continues to be quoted in many different contexts. One day he was asked to visit a slum. He declined and told reporters, "If you've seen one slum, you've seen them all." Hmmm. . . .

Thomas Marshall's Claim to Fame

One day, a reporter asked Thomas Marshall, vice president under Woodrow Wilson, what he thought the country needed. Marshall didn't skip a beat. He responded, "What this country really needs is a good five-cent cigar."

Marshall's remark is still carried in quotation books today and, sadly, critics say he never said or did anything else that anyone can remember.

Before becoming vice president in 1913, Marshall had been governor of Indiana and showed himself to be a man of conflicting opinions: While he promoted progressive social legislation, he was opposed to giving women the right to vote. Maybe it was because he feared they'd vote against five-cent cigars.

Well, Hello, Dolley!

Ever heard of Dolly Madison Ice Cream? It's not just some coincidence that this ice cream company is named after the former first lady (although they dropped the "e" from her name). President James Madison's wife loved to give elaborate dinner parties at the White House, where she served many delicacies, and some historians credit her with introducing ice cream to America.

Ice cream was developed in Italy and France, but it was generally unknown in the U.S. in the early 1800s when Dolley Madison began serving the great new dessert to White House guests. Stories about the wonderfully cold confection soon abounded and its popularity was secured.

Dolley Payne Todd was a twenty-six-year-old widow when she married James Madison, and aside from her famous parties—and ice cream—she's also remembered for removing valuable artwork and papers from the White House for safekeeping before the British invasion of Washington in the War of 1812.

Losing Streak

William Jennings Bryan is the only person in U.S. history to be nominated by a major party to run for president three times—and lose every time. (Oddly, each of Bryan's losses was to a man named William, and Bryan's own name was William.)

The Democrats nominated Bryan in 1896, but he lost to the Republican, William McKinley. The Democrats tried again in 1900, pitting Bryan against McKinley for a second time, but Bryan lost again. After an eight-year hiatus, the Democrats turned to Bryan once more, running him against William Howard Taft in 1908. Bryan made history by losing again.

Bryan was a colorful orator in the U.S. House of Representatives who became nationally famous for his speech against the gold standard, a big issue in 1896. He said, "You shall not crucify mankind upon a cross of gold." Largely because of that "Cross of Gold" speech, Democrats, who wanted to take America off the gold standard, nominated him to run for president, starting his—and their—losing streak.

Bryan's Sad End

Although he was a three-time loser, William Jennings Bryan finally managed to win something. Bryan was a religious fundamentalist who believed in a literal interpretation of the Bible, and this belief led him to his involvement in one of the most famous trials in U.S. history.

In 1925, a Tennessee teacher named John Scopes was arrested for teaching evolution in a public school, which at the time was against state law. His trial captivated America, partially because of the two flamboyant lawyers. Defending Scopes was a prominent criminal lawyer, Clarence Darrow, and prosecuting Scopes was Bryan.

The drama of the trial, which dragged on virtually all summer in a stifling hot, un-air-conditioned courtroom in Dayton, Tennessee, was later captured in the successful Broadway play and subsequent movie *Inherit the Wind*.

In shirtsleeves, Bryan and Darrow battled each other with eloquent speeches about the Bible and religion. Bryan won—but essentially lost the case. Scopes was found guilty, but the penalty against him was just a $100 fine. Bryan, exhausted from the trial and depressed over the outcome, died in Dayton just five days after the verdict.

Following the assassination of JFK, LBJ was sworn in by Judge Sarah Hughes—the first female oath-giver. JFK had appointed her just two years earlier.

FAST FACT

Now That's Good Luck

The first attempted presidential assassination in the U.S. occurred in 1835. A man named Richard Lawrence fired two pistols at Andrew Jackson from only six feet away.

Lawrence was described as a house painter who was mentally ill. According to testimony at his trial, Lawrence thought he was the king of England and the United States. He felt that Jackson, his clerk, was taking too much power away from him. Not surprisingly, Lawrence was found insane and committed to a combination of jail and mental institutions for life.

Lawrence made his assassination attempt at the Capitol rotunda as Jackson was leaving a funeral service for Representative Warren Davis of South Carolina.

So how did he miss if he was just six feet away? It's not that he was a bad aim. Somehow, miraculously, both of Lawrence's pistols misfired, and Jackson was unhurt. Guards later tested the pistols and they fired perfectly. The mystery of the misfiring has never been solved. But you can bet Jackson—and the rest of the nation—was relieved that they did!

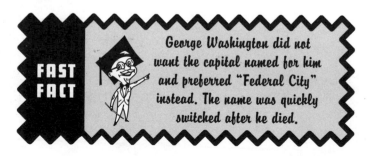

FAST FACT

George Washington did not want the capital named for him and preferred "Federal City" instead. The name was quickly switched after he died.

Who's Buried in Grant's Tomb?

Grant's Tomb, on New York City's Riverside Drive, is an impressive monument honoring President Ulysses Grant. You probably remember that favorite old trick question: "Who's buried in Grant's Tomb?" But the usual answer, Ulysses S. Grant, is only half right. Grant's wife, Julia, is buried there, too.

In fact, it's because of Julia that Grant was entombed in New York City in the first place. Grant wanted his wife to be placed beside him when she died, and was hoping to be buried on the grounds of his alma mater, the U.S. Military Academy at West Point, New York. But regulations at that time prohibited women from being buried at the academy, so the nearest big city was chosen.

New York is happy to have them.

Only two president—vice president pairs have shared the same first name: John Quincy Adams and John Calhoun; and Woodrow Wilson and Thomas Marshall. Wait a second, that can't be right . . . Oh yes, Wilson's real first name was Thomas.

FAST FACT

The First Diverse Ticket

The first female presidential nominee was Victoria Claflin Woodhull of New York. Victoria, an active campaigner for women's rights, was nominated to run for president on the third-party Equal Rights ticket back in 1872.

Her running mate was another first—Frederick Douglass of Massachusetts, the first African American nominated for vice president. Douglass was a well-known antislavery orator and writer before the Civil War, and was appointed U.S. minister to Haiti after the war.

Though the Woodhull-Douglass ticket broke new ground, they couldn't win the uphill battle they faced. Aside from the difficulties of being a third party, they weren't helped by the fact that no woman anywhere in America could vote in a national election at that time (women didn't get the right to vote until 1920) and many African Americans were inhibited from voting in some states because of various local laws that eventually were found to be unconstitutional.

Republican Ulysses Grant won the election.

Mixing Up the Cabinet

None of the first thirty-one presidents had a woman in their cabinets. Finally, in 1933, Franklin Roosevelt appointed the first female cabinet member: Frances Perkins, named secretary of labor.

Previously, Perkins was director of investigations for the New York State Factory Commission and chairman of the New York Industrial Board. She had been instrumental in reducing the workweek for women in her state from fifty-four to forty-eight hours.

While in the cabinet, she headed the President's Committee on Economic Security that laid the groundwork for the nation's first Social Security Act.

The Fight for the Capital

Trenton, New Jersey, almost became our nation's capital.

When congressional delegates met to choose the permanent U.S. capital, Trenton was the favorite because it had served well as a temporary capital during the Revolutionary War.

But as the meeting dragged on, other cities and states started to campaign for the capital to be in their section of the country.

Northern and Southern states could not agree on the right place to park the power.

Finally, Washington, D.C., was selected as a compromise. It worked out well because, at the time,

Washington was about halfway between the North and South.

But had the vote come sooner, the U.S. capital might well have been Trenton.

FAST FACT

Continental divide: Herbert Hoover and his wife, Lucy, were the first president and first lady to be born west of the Mississippi.

The Stuff of Legends

There's hardly an American alive who hasn't heard the story of George Washington chopping down that famous cherry tree. Well, most historians agree that it never really happened. The story is just a myth designed to show how honest Washington was.

That legendary line attributed to young Washington— "Father, I cannot tell a lie"—was actually written by minister and author Mason Weems, who was popular in the late the 1700s and early 1800s.

Weems had a reputation for making up tales to glorify the people he was writing about.

In his book *The Life and Memorable Actions of George Washington*, Weems created yet another legend and had Washington throw a stone across the Rappahannock River. In reality, in the area where George was supposed to have done it, the river is too wide to make such a feat physically possible.

But many people wanted to believe that Washington was super-strong and extra-honest. Thus, Weems's legends became part of American folklore. Now that's what you could call good publicity.

The Real First President

From 1776, when America became independent, until 1789, when George Washington took office for his first term, the Continental Congress ran the nation. In 1781 they elected John Hanson as chairman of the congress and gave him the title of "President of the United States in Congress Assembled."

Some historians argue that Hanson should therefore be considered the first U.S. president.

But other historians point out that although Hanson had the title of president, he really was just the leader of Congress and not of the executive branch.

So, who was Hanson? He was an early supporter of the American cause against Great Britain and was active in politics in his home state of Maryland, where he was a member of his state's legislature. He was then elected to the Continental Congress and, upon being chosen as its head, was often addressed as "Mr. President."

Despite the fun you can have with speculation about whether Hanson was the first U.S. president, Washington's descendants don't need to worry. George Washington's place in history seems secure since Washington was, without question, the first president of the executive branch—and was the first president elected under the Constitution.

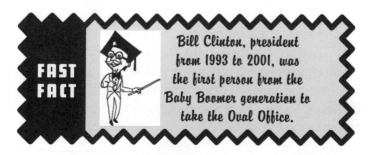

FAST FACT

Bill Clinton, president from 1993 to 2001, was the first person from the Baby Boomer generation to take the Oval Office.

The Turning Point

It all started with a high school trip from Arkansas to Washington, D.C.

When Bill Clinton was a high school senior in 1963, he was picked to make a trip to the White House as part of the American Legion's Boys' Nation group, a youth program designed to teach students about the U.S. government.

It was a lucky day for the Arkansas group when they got to Washington and toured the White House. It just so happened that President John Kennedy was available that day to meet them. Young Bill Clinton had the chance to shake hands and make small talk with the president himself.

When Clinton became president, he was quoted as saying that the meeting with Kennedy altered his life. He had been thinking of becoming a writer, teacher, or musician, but meeting Kennedy left such a deep impression on him that he set his sights on government and politics.

Of course, neither could have known on that summer day in 1963 as Kennedy shook Clinton's hand, that thirty years later, Clinton would be back in the White House—perhaps standing on that same spot—as president of the United States.

Not Just a Girl's Best Friend

Cecil Rhodes left his native England in 1870 for South Africa and eventually controlled almost all the diamonds produced in the world. He acquired most of the diamond mines in Africa and formed the famous De Beers Company to market the diamonds.

Rhodes had a virtual monopoly and made a fortune. He vowed to give some of it back to a worthy cause and chose education because as a young man a lung illness prevented him from enrolling in college.

At the height of his business success in 1900, he decided to fund the annual Rhodes Scholarships that give students two years residence and study at England's prestigious Oxford University.

One of the candidates who won a scholarship in 1968 was a graduate of Georgetown University in Washington, D.C., by the name of Bill Clinton. Clinton is the only U.S. president to have won a Rhodes Scholarship.

After Oxford, Clinton headed to the Yale law school, where he met his fellow student and future wife, Hillary Rodham.

> Only three major American airports are named for presidents: Ronald Reagan National in Washington, the George Bush Intercontinental in Houston, and John F. Kennedy International in New York.

FAST FACT

Lucky Break

Ronald Reagan had no idea that a business trip in 1937 would result in a movie career that would eventually lead him to the governorship of California and the presidency of the United States.

Reagan was just twenty-five years old in 1936 when he worked as a radio announcer at station WHO in Des Moines, Iowa. Among his many duties, Reagan was responsible for re-creating baseball games of the Chicago Cubs from telegraph reports.

The next year the station sent him to cover the Cubs spring training camp. The spring training camp happened to be in the Los Angeles area—and while Reagan was there, a friend urged him to try a screen test.

Reagan was taken to Warner Brothers, where he passed his test and was cast in a movie almost immediately. The film, released in 1937, was *Love is on the Air*, in which Reagan played—appropriately—a radio announcer. That started him on his way to years of movie stardom, the presidency of the Screen Actors' Guild, and spokesman for the General Electric Company, where he made patriotic speeches that caught the eyes and ears of influential Republican backers who ran him for governor—and then, president.

A Good One from the Gip

During his first year as president, on March 30, 1981, Ronald Reagan was shot and wounded by John Hinckley as he walked out of the Hilton Hotel in Washington. Though Reagan was hurt, his funny bone was apparently unharmed. He tried to reassure his wife, Nancy, that he was okay by quoting an old famous line from boxing.

The line comes from the fight between Billy Conn and Joe Louis for the heavyweight championship of the world in 1941. Conn was leading and was on the verge of taking the title away from Louis when Louis unloaded a punch that knocked Conn out in the thirteenth round.

After the fight, Conn explained it to his wife by saying, "Honey, I forgot to duck." And those were the very same words that the Gip used after the failed assassination attempt.

Reagan didn't end his joking there. As he was being wheeled into the operating room at George Washington Hospital for emergency surgery to have the bullet removed from his chest, Reagan looked at his doctors and said, "Please tell me you're all Republicans."

How Low Can You Go?

Can you guess which president had the lowest approval rating in all the years such polling has been made (1936 to the present)?

The answer may surprise you: He was a president who generally had a good image as a decent, highly moral, likeable man. He even won the Nobel Peace Prize. The winner (or loser) in question is Jimmy Carter.

Sadly, during his term in office from 1977 to 1981, Jimmy Carter was dogged by a failing economy, sky-high interest rates (as high as twenty percent), and the holding of American hostages at the U.S. embassy in Iran.

Carter's favorable rating in the Gallup Poll was only twenty-one percent in 1980. Even Richard Nixon, who was pressured to resign the presidency, never had an approval rating that low.

His low approval ruined any chance Carter had to be reelected. Carter didn't let this get him down. After losing to Ronald Reagan in the 1980 election, Carter was honored with the Nobel Peace Prize in 2002 for his efforts to bring peace to the Middle East while he was president and his post-presidential commitment to human rights and promotion of democracy around the world.

"Do You Know Me?"

Jimmy Carter was one of the least-known candidates in modern times when he decided to run for president in 1976. Few people outside his native state of Georgia had ever heard much about him.

Carter was no fool. He jumped on this fact and began to campaign nationally by using a line that eventually became famous: He'd walk up to people and say, "Hi, do you know me? I'm Jimmy Carter, and I'm running for president of the United States."

This might seem exaggerated, but it's not. Jimmy went on the TV show *What's My Line?* early in his campaign, and the blindfolded panel couldn't guess who he was.

None of this seemed to matter, though. By promising to take the moral high road in the period after the Watergate scandal, Carter won the Democratic nomination and defeated President Gerald Ford.

Carter became the first president from the Deep South since before the Civil War. He was a peanut farmer who had served in the Georgia senate and was a one-term governor of Georgia before making his unlikely—but successful—run for president.

Déjà Vu

Shortly after Hillary Rodham graduated from the Yale law school in 1973, she took a job as an attorney for the Children's Defense Fund and then was chosen to be on the inquiry staff of the House of Representatives Judiciary Committee.

And what was the committee working on? The Watergate investigation and possible impeachment of President Richard Nixon.

Little did Hillary know then that her own husband would be facing a very similar situation twenty-four years later.

Hillary married Bill Clinton in 1975, a year after the House Judiciary Committee's work on Nixon was over, and moved with him to Arkansas, where both joined the faculty of the University of Arkansas law school. Bill soon started his political career, winning elections for attorney general and governor of Arkansas, and Hillary entered private law practice. They would enter the White House as president and first lady in 1993.

FAST FACT

Elizabeth Dole won the U.S. Senate seat from North Carolina in 2002 and made history as the first wife of an unsuccessful presidential candidate (Robert Dole) to win an elective office.

Death . . . and Mystery, No. 1

The deaths of three of the eight presidents who passed away in office are veiled in mystery. The first of these, Zachary Taylor, died sixteen months into his presidential term at the age of sixty-five.

The official story goes something like this: Taylor was at the ceremony laying the cornerstone for the Washington Monument on a stifling hot day, July 4, 1850, when he consumed large quantities of iced milk, cold cherries, and pickled cucumbers. He developed gastroenteritis and died from the disease five days later.

But some folks disputed that diagnosis. Some doctors say he died of typhus or cholera, but others think that Taylor was intentionally poisoned by political enemies.

There was some discussion of exhuming his body to test for arsenic, but it was never done. Nothing was ever proved, no one was ever charged, and the actual cause of Taylor's death remains a mystery today.

Mystery No. 2

Warren Harding died on August 2, 1923, at age fifty-seven. He was two years and 151 days into his presidential term.

Harding fell ill shortly before his death. Reports said he had suffered from food poisoning, and then doctors said he had pneumonia. He died a few days later.

Some people said he died from depression and a broken heart because of the scandals in his administration perpetrated by friends he trusted. No autopsy was ever performed and the exact cause of death is still not known.

Perhaps as a result, Harding's wife fell under suspicion. Some said she wanted her husband dead to spare him the grief over the White House scandals. Others said she had found out that Harding had a long-time mistress. But that's not all. Dr. Charles Sawyer, Harding's doctor, died mysteriously one year after Harding. And as was the case with Warren Harding, the only person with Sawyer at the time of his death was . . . Mrs. Harding.

Mystery No. 3

The third controversial presidential death is, of course, the assassination of John Kennedy in 1963.

Several recent surveys show that more than one-half of Americans don't accept the official Warren Commission findings that one gunman, Lee Harvey Oswald, acted alone in the assassination. Instead they think there was some kind of conspiracy at work.

Part of the continuing speculation about a conspiracy involves theories that shots were fired at Kennedy from two directions, which would disprove the one-gunman finding. There are also a bunch of questions about who was behind the assassination. Was it Oswald acting alone, or was it the Soviet Union, Cuba, the Mafia, or some other person or group?

More than forty years have passed, and the Kennedy assassination is perhaps the greatest murder mystery of all time.

Whodunnit? We may never know for sure.

Presidential Ladies

Two women whose initials are A.A. and B.B. share something that sets them apart from all other women throughout history. Can you guess who they are and what they share?

Abigail Adams and Barbara Bush are the only two women in history who were both wives and mothers of U.S. presidents.

Abigail Adams's husband, John, was the second U.S. president, taking office in 1797. Then her son John Quincy became the sixth president when he took office in 1825.

Barbara Bush's husband, George, was elected the forty-first president, going to the White House in 1989, and her son George W. became the forty-third president in 2001.

Each woman has one thing up on the other: Barbara has another son who was elected governor of a U.S. state, Jeb Bush of Florida, and Abigail came close to becoming the only woman whose husband, son, and grandson were presidents. Her grandson Charles was talked about as a possible presidential candidate several times between 1848 to 1872, but never won a nomination. Oh, well.

Success at an Early Age

According to the Constitution, you have to be at least twenty-five years old to serve in the U.S. House of Representatives. While few people try for the job at that age, Bill Clinton came close.

Bill ran for an Arkansas House seat when he was twenty-eight and teaching at the University of Arkansas. Bill didn't win, but he kicked off a meteoric political career that culminated in the White House eighteen years later.

After losing his bid for the House of Representatives, Clinton tried for his state's attorney general office at age thirty and was elected. In 1978, the thirty-two-year-old ran for governor of Arkansas and won, making Clinton the youngest governor in America at that time.

Clinton was elected to five more two-year terms as governor and decided to enter the presidential primaries in 1992, when he was relatively unknown on the national scene. He captured primary after primary by focusing on the economy, which was then in recession, and promising health care reform and tax cuts for the middle class. His primary victories secured the Democratic Party nomination.

Clinton was just forty-six that year when he was elected president, becoming the third youngest president of all time after Theodore Roosevelt (forty-two years old) and John Kennedy (forty-three).

Career Change

Many presidents have been sports fans, but only one owned a team. And we're not talking just any team—this was major league.

In 1989 George W. Bush put together a group of investors and bought big-league baseball's Texas Rangers.

Bush became the managing general partner of the Rangers and stayed in that post until he sold the team in 1994. The Rangers never made the playoffs during Bush's five years at the helm.

Even though Bush didn't have such a great streak, there were rumors that he was considered for the position of commissioner of baseball after Fay Vincent was fired in 1992. Bud Selig, owner of the Milwaukee Brewers, got the job instead.

Bush left the baseball diamond behind and moved on to greener pastures. He tried his luck at politics and ran for governor of Texas in 1994. Bush won and set a new record: He became the first son of a U.S. president to be the governor of a U.S. state.

Presidential Practices

You might not know Al Smith's name, but he made history when he was chosen by the Democrats to run against Herbert Hoover in 1928. Smith became the first non-Protestant ever nominated for U.S. president by a major party.

Smith, a Catholic, had been a popular governor of New York elected to four terms, but that wasn't enough to win him the presidency. Hoover beat him with a big margin of more than six million votes.

Religious prejudice against Smith was a factor in his loss, just as it would be the next time a Catholic ran for president, thirty-two years later. John Kennedy had to face such questions in 1960 as whether his first allegiance would be to the pope or to the people of the United States. Kennedy won the election (over Richard Nixon) and became the first Catholic president, but many political experts said his close margin of victory, 34,227,096 votes to Nixon's 34,107,646, would have been greater if not for his Catholicism.

Religion seems less of an issue in the twenty-first century. Four Catholics were announced candidates for the 2004 election—John Kerry, Dennis Kucinich, Carol Braun, and Wesley Clark. Clark, a practicing Catholic as an adult, is the son of a Jewish father. And Joe Lieberman became the first Jewish person ever nominated to run for vice president when he was chosen as Al Gore's running mate in 2000, and he then became a candidate for president in 2004.

First Leading Lady

Nancy Reagan never came close to having the film career her husband did, but she did manage to appear in eleven Hollywood movies. She was even billed as the leading lady in the 1957 film *Hellcats of the Navy*—the only movie in which she costarred with her husband, Ronald Reagan.

Nancy Reagan was born Nancy Robbins in New York in 1921. Her parents divorced shortly after she was born. Her mother, a stage actress named Edith, married a neurosurgeon named Loyal Davis when Nancy was seven. And Davis was the name Nancy went by until she married Reagan.

Nancy majored in drama at Smith College and then set off for Broadway, where she acted in a few plays, including the hit musical *Lute Song*. A Hollywood offer followed and she acted in the movies from 1949 to 1957. Nancy met Reagan in 1951 and she married the future prez the next year.

Presidential Precedent

The oath that every U.S. president must take when being sworn into office is in Article II of the Constitution. In keeping with the Constitution's advocacy of separation of church and state, there is no mention of God or religion in the oath. But thanks to an ad-lib by one president, all that changed.

The oath, as it appears in the Constitution, is:

"I do solemnly swear (or affirm) that I will faithfully execute the office of President of the United States, and will, to the best of my ability, preserve, protect and defend the Constitution of the United States."

When George Washington spoke the oath at his first inauguration in 1789, he tacked on four words at the end— "So help me God"—and that has become an unofficial custom. Every president since then has added those words, adding one more thing to the long list of George Washington's legacies.

But that's not all. Although there's no mention of it in the Constitution, every president has placed his left hand on a Bible and raised his right hand while taking the oath.

Famous Last Words

President John Kennedy was not alone on the fateful day of November 23, 1963, as he rode through the streets of Dallas in a motorcade. In the car with him were his wife, Jackie; a Secret Service man; the governor of Texas, John Connally; and Connally's wife, Nellie.

The Connallys, as host to the president, wanted to make sure he was enjoying his trip. There had been some opposition to Kennedy among Texas Democrats who had said they would not support him for a second term, so Kennedy was in Texas to try to heal the split in the party. He was in Dallas because the city was known to be the center of anti-Kennedy feelings.

Governor and Mrs. Connally were happy to see that mostly friendly, cheering crowds lined the streets for Kennedy's motorcade. As their car approached Dealey Plaza, Nellie Connally turned around from her front seat and said to Kennedy, "You can't say Dallas doesn't love you, Mr. President." It was just at that moment that the shots rang out.

Those were the last words Kennedy ever heard.

And Then What?

Did you ever wonder who would serve if neither the president nor the vice president could? If there is neither a president nor vice president by reason of death, resignation, inability to perform, or removal from office, then the Speaker of the House of Representatives is the next in line.

If there is no Speaker, or if the Speaker fails to qualify (he/she must be at least thirty-five years old, a natural-born citizen, and a U.S. resident for at least fourteen years), the job falls next to the president pro tempore of the Senate (usually the senior member of the Senate in years of service).

If the president pro tempore cannot serve, there begins a line that runs through the president's cabinet, starting with the secretary of state, then going to the secretaries of the treasury and defense, the attorney general, secretaries of the interior, agriculture, commerce, labor, housing and urban development, transportation, energy, health and human services, education, veterans affairs, and homeland security.

It's a long list, but as you might have guessed, it's not random. So what's behind the order? The succession of the cabinet members is based on the order in which the departments were created.

The Advisory Board

Surprisingly, the men who wrote the U.S. Constitution established the executive branch of the government, but neglected to include anything about a cabinet for the president.

When George Washington took office in his first term, he realized the mistake the framers (of which he was one) made. He quickly saw the need for advisors and heads of executive departments, so he tapped some heavyweights. He asked Thomas Jefferson to be his secretary of state and Alexander Hamilton to be the secretary of the treasury.

Congress got into the act and passed legislation authorizing the hiring and paying of cabinet members. Congress also made sure it stayed involved: It passed a law saying the president could choose his cabinet, but each choice had to be approved by the Senate. And that's a law that still exists today.

Originally there were only four cabinet posts (secretaries of state, treasury, and war, and the attorney general), but Congress and the president have created more over the years, with the total reaching fifteen by the year 2003. As of 2003, cabinet members are paid $171,900 a year, just slightly less than the vice president, who gets $198,600. Not too shabby.

Baa, Baa, Black Sheep

You might expect to see pets like cats or dogs at the White House, but what about sheep? If you'd come by during Woodrow Wilson's term, that's exactly what you would have found.

During World War I, the head White House groundskeeper and several other gardeners left for military service. Rather than hiring replacements or doing the work himself, President Woodrow Wilson came up with what he considered a brilliant idea.

He ordered that a herd of sheep be brought to the White House to graze on the grass. Not only did the sheep keep the grass short at low cost to taxpayers, but their wool was shorn and sold. Sales of the White House wool raised more than $100,000, which was donated to the Red Cross.

Unfortunately Wilson's good idea took a slightly negative turn when the sheep started eating more of the White House grounds than just the grass. Still, Wilson felt the good outweighed the bad, and the sheep continued to roam the White House lawn for the duration of the war. Now that must have been quite a sight.

Grunge Look

Zachary Taylor wasn't called "Old Rough and Ready" for nothing.

Taylor, the twelfth U.S. president, was a gruff, tough career army man who got his nickname from his troops.

Taylor apparently didn't care much about looks. He often wore messy, dirty clothes—even when he was president. The habit started when he was on the front lines, leading troops in the War of 1812, the Indian wars, and the Mexican War. It was his victory as a general in the Mexican War in 1847 that made Taylor a national hero and catapulted him into the presidency.

Besides not caring about looks, Taylor also had little interest in politics. The first time he voted was when he himself ran for president in 1848.

Taylor's plunge into political life didn't last long. Old Rough and Ready died in the White House from an undisclosed illness at age sixty-five—just one year and 127 days into his presidency.

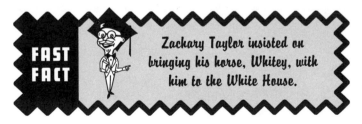

FAST FACT

Zachary Taylor insisted on bringing his horse, Whitey, with him to the White House.

Texas BBQ

Laura Welch grew up in Midland, Texas, and went to Southern Methodist University for a bachelor's degree in education. After several years of teaching in public schools in Dallas and Houston, Ms. Welch enrolled at the University of Texas for a master's degree in library science. That led her to Austin, Texas, where she took a job as a librarian and, at a barbecue one evening in 1977, met George W. Bush.

George must have really impressed her, because he and Laura were married just three months after meeting that night. Four years later, Laura gave birth to twin girls who were named after their two grandmothers—Jenna, for Laura's mother, and Barbara, for George's mother. And twenty years after that, George became president and Laura the first lady.

Church and State

Although each of the first forty-two U.S. presidents considered themselves Christians, three were not members of any church.

The three without any specific affiliation were Thomas Jefferson, Abraham Lincoln, and Andrew Johnson.

Of the other thirty-nine presidents, eleven were Episcopalian, seven Presbyterian, five Baptist, four Unitarian, three Methodist, three Disciples of Christ,

two Quaker, two Dutch Reformed, one Congrega-
tionalist, and one Catholic.

And three presidents were sons of clergymen:
Chester Arthur's father was a Baptist minister; Grover
Cleveland's was a Congregational minister; and
Woodrow Wilson's was a Presbyterian minister.

A Stately Namesake

Grover Cleveland's father, the Rev. Richard Cleveland, was a relative of Moses Cleaveland, the founder
of Cleveland, Ohio, who established the first permanent settlement there. For reasons unknown to
us, both the city and the Reverend dropped the first
a from their name.

The Rail Splitter

Abraham Lincoln's private secretary, John Hay, kept
a diary describing Lincoln's daily habits. In it, he mar-
veled at how little the sixteenth president ate.

According to Hay's account, Lincoln would have
one egg, one piece of toast, and a cup of coffee for

breakfast. For lunch, he'd have just a biscuit and a glass of milk; in the summer he might have just a few grapes instead.

Lincoln usually had dinner between 5:00 and 6:00 P.M., eating, as Hay wrote, "less than anyone I know. He was very abstemious."

Aside from coffee and milk, Lincoln apparently never drank anything but water. Hay reported that it wasn't a matter of principle that kept Lincoln away from alcoholic beverages, it was just that he didn't like them.

It's not surprising that Lincoln was thin given his sparse eating. He was the tallest president, standing six feet four inches, but weighed less than 180 pounds. One of Lincoln's nicknames was "The Rail Splitter," which he earned from one of his jobs as a boy splitting logs for fence rails. The name seemed even more appropriate for the adult Lincoln, who was thin as a rail.

That Famous Beard

Ever see a picture of Abraham Lincoln without a beard? We can all thank Grace Bedell, an eleven-year-old girl from Westfield, New York, for the addition of those famous whiskers.

Lincoln was clean shaven when he made his bid for the presidency in 1860. But little Grace Bedell had a plan. She wrote to Lincoln, "You would look better if you would let your whiskers grow because your face is so thin. All the ladies like whiskers and they would tease their husbands to vote for you and then you would be president."

At a campaign stop near Grace's hometown, Lincoln told the assembled crowd about the letter and asked if the girl was there. She came forward and Lincoln picked her up and kissed her—even though he still had not taken her advice.

Lincoln was elected president without the whiskers. But soon into his first term, he began to grow his famous beard (and interestingly, became the first president to sport one). Seems some of his advisors sided with Grace and said he'd look more dignified with facial hair. Maybe Lincoln agreed with them, because he wore a beard for the rest of his life.

One After the Other

Surprisingly, only two men in the 227 years from 1776 through 2003 have ever been elected to the U.S.

House of Representatives, the U.S. Senate, the U.S. vice presidency, and the U.S. presidency. What's even weirder, they were consecutive presidents.

Lyndon Johnson was elected to the House in 1937, to the Senate in 1948, vice president in 1960, and president in 1964.

Richard Nixon was elected to the House in 1946, to the Senate in 1950, VP in 1952, and president in 1968.

Three of the first ten presidents—
Thomas Jefferson, James
Monroe and John Tyler—graduated
from William & Mary College
in Williamsburg, Virginia.

FAST FACT

That Famous Electoral College

True or false: A person could be elected president even if no one at all voted for him or her in thirty-nine of the fifty states? It's hard to believe, but it's true.

Based on the U.S. Electoral College system, a candidate can be elected by getting the most votes in just the eleven biggest states. If the candidate carries those eleven states, it doesn't matter what happens in the other thirty-nine smaller states.

To win the presidency, a person must have 270 electoral votes, the majority of the 538 members of the Electoral College. States are assigned electoral votes on the basis of how many senators and representatives they have in Congress. All states have two senators, but the number of representatives is determined by a state's population. The bigger the population, the more representatives.

Thus, if a candidate carries California (fifty-five electoral votes), Texas (thirty-four), New York (thirty-one), Florida (twenty-seven), Illinois (twenty-two), Pennsylvania (twenty-one), Ohio (twenty), Michigan (seventeen), New Jersey (fifteen), Georgia (fifteen), and North Carolina (fifteen), the other thirty-nine states wouldn't be a factor in the election. So much for "every vote counts."

FAST FACT

Washington & Jefferson College in Washington, Pennsylvania, is the only college named for two presidents.

Hatching Chickens

Poor Benjamin Wade got ahead of himself when President Andrew Johnson was impeached by the House of Representatives in 1868. It seemed a sure bet that Johnson would be convicted by the Senate and removed from office, and that Benjamin Wade of Ohio, the president pro tempore of the Senate, would succeed him.

Wade was so sure that he would become president of the United States that he began making arrangements and selecting his cabinet. At the same time, the senators started casting their ballots either for or against Johnson's conviction. There was no question about Wade's vote. He didn't like Johnson's post–Civil War reconstruction policies—and he wanted to be president.

But much to Wade's chagrin and surprise, Johnson was acquitted by the margin of just one vote. Johnson continued his presidency and Wade went home after his term a brokenhearted man. It just goes to show, you should never count your chickens before they hatch.

Legal Eagles

More than half of the men who served as president from 1789 to 2003 were lawyers by trade. John Kennedy,

Harry Truman, Ronald Reagan, Theodore Roosevelt, and George Washington were just a few who weren't.

The other non-lawyers who have been president are the two George Bushes, Jimmy Carter, Lyndon Johnson, Dwight Eisenhower, Herbert Hoover, Warren Harding, Ulysses Grant, Andrew Johnson, Zachary Taylor, and William Henry Harrison.

Twenty-six presidents were lawyers: John Adams, Thomas Jefferson, James Madison, James Monroe, John Quincy Adams, Andrew Jackson, Martin Van Buren, John Tyler, James Polk, Millard Fillmore, Franklin Pierce, James Buchanan, Abraham Lincoln, Rutherford Hayes, James Garfield, Chester Arthur, Grover Cleveland, Benjamin Harrison, William McKinley, William Howard Taft, Woodrow Wilson, Calvin Coolidge, Franklin Roosevelt, Richard Nixon, Gerald Ford and Bill Clinton.

No. 1 Cherry Street

All presidents have lived at 1600 Pennsylvania Avenue, except one. He lived at 1 Cherry Street. Can you guess who?

Back when George Washington was inaugurated as the first U.S. president in 1789, the White House was not built and the nation's capital wasn't Washington,

D.C. New York City was the capital at the time, and that's where Washington lived and governed.

The first presidential mansion was located, strangely enough, on Cherry Street—but the street didn't get its name because of Washington's legendary connection with the fruit trees. It was called Cherry Street long before Washington moved there.

It was just a coincidence that that's where Washington set up shop. The home at No. 1 Cherry Street, which was converted into the presidential mansion, was loaned to the nation by Samuel Osgood, president of the National City Bank of New York.

Thomas Jefferson started the presidential custom of shaking hands with fellow Americans; Washington and Adams preferred to bow instead.

FAST FACT

Curious George

You might not believe it, but every head of state of America for almost 100 years was named George.

From 1714 to 1776, when America was a British colony, King George I, II, and III ruled America. Then, by coincidence, the first U.S. president was also named George. George Washington led America until 1797.

After all those years of Georges, there were no other Georges in the presidency until George H. W. Bush in 1989.

Second Fiddle

What do George Clinton, Daniel Tompkins, Richard Johnson, George Dallas, Hannibal Hamlin, Henry Wilson, Thomas Hendricks, Garrett Hobart, and Charles Dawes have in common in regards to American history?

Few people today recognize their names, but they were all vice presidents of the United States.

FAST FACT

Franklin Roosevelt was the only president with three different vice presidents: John Nance Garner, Henry Wallace, and Harry Truman.

Liberty and Death, Yes; Official Post, No

Patrick Henry earned fame with his stirring 1775 speech urging independence from England. His famous words, "I know not what course others may take; but as for me, give me liberty or give me death!" continue to ring through history.

That's not Henry's only claim to fame, though. After America won its freedom and became an independent nation, Henry set an all-time record for turning down high-level jobs that could conceivably have brought him even more fame and even the presidency.

President George Washington wanted to make Henry his secretary of state. Henry said no. Washington offered him posts as minister to Spain or France. Henry said no. Next came an offer to be Chief Justice of the Supreme Court. Henry said no. Finally he was asked to fill a U.S. Senate seat. Yup, you guessed it: Henry said no.

If Henry had accepted Washington's job offers and remained on the national scene, he might have one day been president. (Washington's eventual secretary of state, Thomas Jefferson, did become president.) So why on earth did Henry keep declining?

Years of public service in Virginia before and during the Revolutionary War left Henry badly in debt.

His only way out, he felt, was to establish a private law practice where his reputation would bring him many clients. He did well, but historians will always wonder what would have become of Henry if he had said yes.

Lincoln's Choices

On the eve of the U.S. Civil War, President Abraham Lincoln chose Robert E. Lee as the commander of the Union forces. Lincoln's choice seemed logical enough—Lee graduated with high honors from the U.S. Military Academy at West Point and had served in the U.S. Army for thirty-six years. Fellow general Winfield Scott called him "the greatest military genius in America."

But Lee didn't take Lincoln up on his offer. He said that he could not take the job as Union commander because of his Southern roots. Lee, a native of Virginia, said that although he opposed slavery, he could not fight against the South.

Later, of course, Lee took command of the Southern forces. Lincoln had to make another choice for the leader of the North and selected Ulysses Grant. Thus, Lincoln became the only head of a nation in history to pick men who would be commanders on opposite sides in the same war.

Super Tuesday

Ever wonder why presidential elections are held in November? We can thank Congress for that. The U.S. Constitution gave Congress the right to set the dates for presidential elections and they picked November. Congress thought it was a practical choice: Back then the young nation was largely a rural, farming country and Congress thought early November was the best time because harvesting would be over and winter would not yet have made northern roads impassable.

At any other time, farmers were either too busy or it was too hard for them to reach the polls. Even though things have changed a lot since then, Congress has kept election day on the first Tuesday after the first Monday in November out of custom and tradition.

Many other countries hold elections on Sundays, figuring that's a good day for people to go to the polls since most don't have weekday work schedules to contend with. But that idea never had a chance in Congress. Lobbying by religious groups opposed to worldly activities on Sundays has prevented any move from Tuesdays.

The Pledge Precedent

Time was when nary a day at school began without the Pledge of Allegiance. The custom was initiated somewhat unintentionally by President Harrison in 1892, when he ordered the nation's schools to take part in a one-day celebration of the 400th anniversary of Columbus's voyage to America. As an afterthought, Harrison said part of the festivities should include the recitation of a pledge that had just been written by Francis Bellamy and published by the New England weekly *Youth's Companion*.

The special celebration came and went, but schools continued to have students say the Pledge every morning and the tradition was born.

The Right (Write) Man for the Job

The Continental Congress had a fairly easy time deciding that America should formally declare its independence in June 1776. The tougher part was deciding who was best equipped to write a declaration of independence and express the democratic principles envisioned for this new country.

The chosen one was a brilliant thirty-three-year-old political thinker from Virginia by the name of Thomas Jefferson. Working night and day in a hot, stuffy room, Jefferson wrote one of the greatest landmark documents in history in just two and a half weeks. He was given the assignment on June 11. He finished it and sent it to Congress on June 28. They approved it on July 2 and declared it on July 4.

What Security?

Things were really different when Thomas Jefferson was inaugurated for his first term as president. On that big day, March 4, 1801, Jefferson left the boardinghouse where he was staying and walked to the

Capitol for the inauguration ceremonies. The only people accompanying him were some well-wishers— there were no Secret Service, no guards, no security at all.

That's just how it was back then. It's hard to believe, but when visitors came to the White House in those days, the president would often answer the door himself.

It wasn't until Andrew Jackson was in office in the 1830s that presidents had a bodyguard on a regular basis. That followed an assassination attempt on Jackson, the first such attempt in American history. But there was still no Secret Service directing presidential security on a formal basis.

The Secret Service, originally created to catch counterfeiters in the 1860s, was finally put in full-time charge of protecting the president, his immediate family, the vice president, and president-elect in 1901, after the assassination of William McKinley.

Wagging the Dog

Today we often complain about the media's growing role in politics, but it isn't a new one. In many ways, the media was the cause of the Spanish-American War of the late 1800s.

During that time there was unrest in Cuba because Cubans were resisting the Spanish rule that governed the island. There were increasing reports of Spanish mistreatment of Cubans and some Americans wanted the U.S. to intervene, but President William McKinley feared risking American lives and was reluctant to send in troops. However, flamboyant newspaper publisher William Randolph Hearst wanted that situation—and the American stance on the war—to change.

Hearst's *New York Journal* was in a circulation battle against Joseph Pulitzer's *New York World*. Hearst began printing sensational, exaggerated reports of atrocities in Cuba to whip up circulation for his paper. Then he sent artist Frederic Remington to Cuba to sketch the skirmishes. When Remington got to Cuba, he didn't find much fighting and asked to return. Hearst cabled his famous reply: "You furnish the pictures and I'll furnish the war."

Hearst kept pounding away (and selling more newspapers). The American public, and members of Congress, began demanding that the U.S. declare war on Spain and free Cuba. Then an American battleship, the *Maine*, blew up in Havana's harbor. To this day no one knows the cause of the explosion, but it was the tipping point that led to the Spanish-American War.

The Truth Behind the Legend

Future president Theodore Roosevelt gained national fame and popularity when his Rough Riders charged up San Juan Hill in a decisive battle of the Spanish-American War in 1898.

But who were the Rough Riders, and what did they ride? Although Roosevelt's unit was part of the cavalry, they did not ride on horses for their famous charge. There was no room for their horses on the ship carrying them to Cuba for the war, so the Rough Riders fought on foot.

And despite what the legend says, they did not charge up San Juan Hill. The Rough Riders went up Kettle Hill, a smaller hill in front of San Juan Hill, and fired from there on the Spaniards, who were on San Juan Hill.

None of these little facts seemed to matter, though. Roosevelt became a popular hero and was the choice for vice president, running with President McKinley in the 1900 election. They won, and when McKinley was assassinated a year later, Roosevelt became president.

Hardworking T. R.

President Theodore Roosevelt knew how to keep himself busy.

The son of a wealthy father from New York City, Roosevelt was a man of great energy who decided early to dedicate himself to what he called "the strenuous life." In between serving in the New York state assembly and as governor of New York, Roosevelt headed to North Dakota and tried his hand as a rancher. He ran two ranches in fourteen- and sixteen-hour days.

Besides that, he was president of the New York City Board of Police Commissioners, a member of the U.S. Civil Service Commission, assistant secretary of the navy, leader of the Rough Riders in the Spanish-American War, and a lieutenant colonel in the army.

And that was all by the time he was just forty-two years old. At age forty-two, Roosevelt became vice president and then president of the United States.

He won the Nobel Peace Prize for helping settle the Russo-Japanese War and became the first president to ride in an airplane, an automobile, and a submarine. After leaving the presidency, he was a big-game hunter in Africa and led scientific expeditions for the Smithsonian Institution while also becoming a writer. There wasn't much that Roosevelt didn't do!

Good Intentions

When special visitors come to the White House, the president is usually briefed in advance so that he can think of something nice and appropriate to say. Sometimes, unfortunately, it doesn't work out that way.

One day in 1925, the famous All-American football player Red Grange was brought to the White House to meet President Calvin Coolidge. Grange had just finished a spectacular career at the University of Illinois and had joined the Chicago Bears of the National Football League. Coolidge's advisers thought it would be good publicity to have newspapers publish a picture of the president standing with a football hero.

The problem was that Coolidge knew little about football and had no idea who the Chicago Bears were in the then relatively new NFL. Coolidge congratulated Grange for joining the Chicago Bears—as he had been briefed to do—but then added, "I've always liked bear acts." Oops.

Babe Ruth met President Coolidge on a stifling hot day in the mid-1920s and said, "Christ, it's hot, ain't it, Prez?"

FAST FACT

Way to Go, Ike!

One of the biggest upsets in the history of the U.S. Army happened when Dwight Eisenhower was picked ahead of many more-senior officers to lead Allied armies to victory in Europe in World War II.

Ike wasn't even a general right before the war. In fact, he wasn't even made a full colonel until 1941, the year the U.S. entered the war. But in 1941, he led war games in Louisiana and his maneuvers in the exercises caught the eye of the army chief of staff, General George Marshall.

That catapulted him forward on his meteoric rise from obscurity to superstardom. Just six months after being made a colonel, Eisenhower was promoted to brigadier general and given the assignment of charting an Allied invasion of Europe. Three days after submitting his plan, he was named commander of American forces in Europe. He had been advanced over 366 senior officers for the job.

On June 6, D-Day, Ike led all the Allied forces to the beginning of the end of World War II in Europe. On that day he solidified his place as an American hero and a popular president-to-be.

FAST FACT

Dwight Eisenhower didn't realize to whom he was speaking when, as a bit of small talk, he asked President Cleveland's widow where she'd lived while in Washington. Somewhat stunned, Mrs. Cleveland responded, "Why, in the White House, of course."

Nixon and Eisenhower, Together Again

When Julie Nixon and David Eisenhower got married, they made history.

Twenty-year-old Julie Nixon was the younger daughter of Richard Nixon; David Eisenhower was the only grandson of Dwight Eisenhower. Their marriage marked the only time in U.S. history that the grandson of one president married the daughter of another.

The American-style "royal wedding" took place on December 22, 1968, when Julie's father was president-elect, and David's grandfather was in retirement after leaving the presidency in 1961.

Never before had two presidential families been united so closely by marriage. Julie and David got to know each other when David's future father-in-law was the vice president and his grandfather was the president.

Despite their backgrounds, neither Julie nor David went into politics. Julie became active in social work and David became a writer (he authored a well-regarded biography of his grandfather) and a teacher.

The Big White House

It might not look that big from the outside, but the White House has 132 rooms, thirty-five bathrooms, twenty-eight fireplaces, eight staircases, and three elevators.

It didn't start off that spacious when it was built in 1800. The main additions have been the West Wing, completed in 1902, that now contains the president's office and cabinet room, and the East Wing, finished in 1942, that provided more office space and a room for the press.

Legend has it that Teddy Roosevelt had the West Wing built for his office so that while he was working he could have some privacy from his six rambunctious children who romped through the main part of the White House.

But office space hasn't been the only thing added. Presidents have made renovations over the years to include an indoor swimming pool, indoor tennis court, a jogging track, bowling lane, and a movie theater.

Let's Make a Deal

Thomas Jefferson was a big spender. As noted earlier, his lavish style of living left him in deep personal debt. He spent a lot of money on rare, expensive books, fine imported wines, and extravagant entertaining. And he also made the biggest real estate deal of all time for his country.

Jefferson convinced the French in 1803 to sell all the land they controlled west of the Mississippi River to the United States. At the time, the French were preoccupied with the Napoleonic wars in Europe; since they didn't want to engage in battle in America, too, they were happy to sell.

The U.S. borrowed $15 million from English and Dutch banks to buy the land in what became known as the Louisiana Purchase.

So how big was Jefferson's real estate deal? He doubled the size of the United States, buying more than 800,000 square miles and giving the country land that became all or part of fifteen states—Arkansas, Colorado, Iowa, Kansas, Louisiana, Minnesota, Missouri, Montana, Nebraska, New Mexico, North Dakota, Oklahoma, South Dakota, Texas, and Wyoming. Now that's some deal.

Good president, Bad Teeth

Poor George Washington. He may have been one of the greatest presidents with one of the worst sets of dentures.

Washington lost all his natural teeth by the time he was elected president and never seemed able to get good replacements. He tried many different sets of dentures, including some made of rhinoceros horns, wood, whalebone, and even deer antlers, but none were right.

Paul Revere of Midnight Ride fame, who was a silversmith and craftsman by trade, made a set of false teeth for George. But even those were not a good fit.

Washington often complained of discomfort when it came to his dentures and spoke with a clicking sound. Some critics said Washington always had a sour look because of the problems with his teeth.

Ironically, he took amazing care of his horses' teeth, ordering that they be brushed every morning.

Lucky One

When the president delivers the State of the Union message every year in the chambers of the House of Representatives, everybody at the highest levels of government is usually there—all members of Congress, the vice president, Supreme Court justices, the military chiefs of staff, and the president's cabinet—but one person is politely told to stay away.

That one cabinet member is sent to an undisclosed location away from the Capitol building.

The tradition began when someone realized it wasn't a good idea to put all of the top officials under one roof at one time. Sounds like a logical thought, but it's still a bit curious. The U.S. government would have a difficult time functioning if disaster struck that building while almost everyone was there. But it would be especially difficult for one lonely cabinet member to reconstruct the government on his own.

The Times, They Are A-changing

You'd think if any president had headed a labor union, he probably would have been a liberal Democrat. But then you'd be wrong.

The only U.S. president who had also been a president of a union was a man who was a conservative Republican in the White House (and fired striking members of the air traffic controllers union). That man was Ronald Reagan.

In his Hollywood days, before being elected governor of California and president of the United States, Reagan headed the Screen Actors' Guild for seven years in the 1940s and '50s. He led the union during tumultuous times when actors were facing both the breakup of the studio system with the loss of guaranteed contracts, and the hearings by the House Un-American Activities Committee on possible infiltration of communists in the film industry.

Back then, the future conservative U.S. president was considered a liberal. Boy, times sure do change.

FAST FACT

While a student at Yale law school in the 1930s, Gerald Ford took modeling jobs for the covers of *Cosmopolitan* and *Look* magazines.

The First Hostess

Dolley Madison, the wife of President James Madison, served as White House hostess for sixteen years. How did she manage that feat when her husband wasn't president for that long?

When Thomas Jefferson became president in 1801, he had already been a widower for eighteen years. With no wife to serve as first lady, he asked Dolley Madison, the wife of his secretary of state, James Madison, to be the hostess at White House functions.

So Dolley Madison graciously performed hostess duties for the eight years Jefferson was president. Then her own husband was elected president, succeeding Jefferson, and was in office for eight years, from 1809 to 1817. And that is how Dolley racked up a total of sixteen years as "first hostess."

Harry Truman and Arthur Eisenhower were roommates and colleagues in Kansas. Forty years later, Harry would be president and would be succeeded by Arthur's brother, Ike.

FAST FACT

Fathers and Sons

You would think that when there was a father-son combination serving as U.S. presidents, there would be a relatively long time lapse between their admin-istrations—but that's not the case with George H. W. and George W. Bush. In fact, only one president served between them.

George H.W. became president at age sixty-four in 1989. He left office in 1993 when Bill Clinton suc-ceeded him. The very next president after Clinton was George W., who began his term in 2001 at age fifty-four. The elder Bush is just twenty-two years older than his son.

There were more years between the presidencies of the only other father-son combination. John Adams was president from 1797 to 1801. Then came three presidents who all served eight-year terms—Thomas Jefferson, James Madison and James Monroe. Adams's son, John Quincy, took office twenty-four years after his father, in 1825, and served until 1829.

Name Change?

We all know that George Washington fought the British in the Revolutionary War. But what you may not know is that his famous home, Mt. Vernon, is named after a British military officer.

Mt. Vernon, which lies about fifteen miles south of Washington, D.C., was built by George's half brother, Lawrence, in 1743. Lawrence named it Mt. Vernon after a British admiral, Edward Vernon, who was an old friend of the Washington family and Lawrence's former commander in the British navy.

When Lawrence died in 1752, he left the home to his wife and daughter. Just eight years later, both of them had died and George inherited Mt. Vernon.

The home became a national shrine in 1853 when the Mt. Vernon Ladies' Association raised money to maintain and administer it. The tombs of George Washington and his wife, Martha, are on the grounds, and the house has been restored to its original 1700s glory.

> *George Washington came down with smallpox at nineteen and carried scars on his face from then on.*
>
> **FAST FACT**

Big Winner, Big Loser

Talk about a fall from grace. One president was a record-setting winner going into the White House and a record-setting loser going out.

When Herbert Hoover won the presidential election in 1928 over Al Smith, he amassed the largest majority of electoral votes ever received by a candidate up to that time. He got 444 electoral votes to Smith's 87—a difference of 357. No other president had ever won by that big a margin.

But that was not the case four years later when Hoover tried for a second term and ran against Franklin Roosevelt. He lost by a new record margin of 413 electoral votes. In that 1932 election, Roosevelt received 472 electoral votes while Hoover got only 59.

Hoover's big loss didn't come as such a surprise. The country was in the throes of the Great Depression, which started during his term. Ironically, Hoover was one of the richest of all U.S. presidents. His wife, Lou Henry Hoover, was the daughter of a wealthy banker, and Hoover himself had become a self-made millionaire as an international mining engineer before entering politics.

Eyes on the Prize

Three U.S. presidents have been awarded the Nobel Peace Prize.

Theodore Roosevelt was not only the first president to win it, but he was also the first American so honored. Roosevelt won the prize in 1906 for mediating the peace treaty between Russia and Japan to end the Russo-Japanese War. He brought both sides together to talk peace at a resort hotel in Portsmouth, New Hampshire.

The second president to win the Nobel Peace Prize was Woodrow Wilson in 1919 for planning the League of Nations at the end of World War I. The League of Nations was supposed to prevent future wars, but it failed in the 1930s.

And in 2002, Jimmy Carter became the third president to win the Nobel Peace Prize, "for his efforts to bring peace to the Middle East during his presidency, and for his post-presidential work for human rights and the promotion of democratic values around the world."

The first Boy Scout to become a U.S. president was John Kennedy in 1961.

FAST FACT

Breaking a Leg

After shooting President Abraham Lincoln on April 14, 1865, at Ford's Theatre in Washington, John Wilkes Booth jumped from the president's box onto the stage. Booth caught his foot on the flag draped in front of the box, fell awkwardly, and broke his leg. Booth was able to limp across the stage, exit through a back door, and escaped on horseback.

The weird thing is not only that Booth tripped over an American flag, but that he was a prominent actor who did, indeed, "break a leg." Considering he was hunted down and shot dead in a Virginia barn twelve days later, maybe it wasn't such good luck.

FAST FACT

A wounded Abraham Lincoln was brought to a boarding house near Ford's Theatre and died in the very same bed where John Wilkes Booth had once slept.

The Skinny on Every Presidential Election

1789
–
2000

1789 . . .

It was no contest. **George Washington** was elected unanimously, getting every Electoral College vote for president. (There was no popular voting then. State legislatures picked the members of the Electoral College.) After his success in the Revolutionary War and leadership in framing the Constitution, along with his personal character and image, there seemed to be no question that Washington was the man to serve as first president.

1792 . . .

Much like the first election, **George Washington** was chosen unanimously for a second term—but not everyone was satisfied with the policies of Washington's Federalist Party, which advocated a strong central government. A minority party, called the Anti-Federalists, that favored more states' rights, began to emerge. They were too weak to challenge Washington, but they would be heard from in future elections.

1796 . . .

After Washington declined to run for a third term,

the Federalists turned to his vice president, **John Adams,** as their candidate. The country had its first real contest for the presidency with the Anti-Federalists selecting Thomas Jefferson to oppose Adams. The electoral vote was close, with Adams beating Jefferson 71–68.

1800 . . .

If you think the 2000 election was strange, this one was even more so. Both **Thomas Jefferson** and Aaron Burr got the same number of electoral votes. The election had ended in an exact tie, the only time that's ever happened. The issue was thrown into the House of Representatives for a decision. The House voted Jefferson president and Burr vice president. The incumbent president, John Adams, who finished third in the electoral votes, was denied a second term and bitterly left office. Adams didn't agree with Jefferson's policies and they remained political enemies until late in their lives when they reconciled with mutual respect.

1804 . . .

Thomas Jefferson easily won a second term, beating

the weakening Federalist Party's candidate, Charles Pinckney, who had been a delegate to the Constitutional Convention. Jefferson's party by this time had changed its name from Anti-Federalist to Democratic-Republican. The electoral vote was 162 to 14 in favor of Jefferson, a whopping margin of 92.05 percent for Jefferson to 7.95 percent for Pinckney.

1808 . . .

Following the lead of George Washington, Thomas Jefferson refused to run for a third term. His party nominated Jefferson's secretary of state, **James Madison**, to run for president. The Federalists again turned to the man who was badly beaten in the previous election, Charles Pinckney. Madison won fairly easily, beating Pinckney 122–89 in the electoral votes.

1812 . . .

Five months before the election, the U.S. declared war on England and the War of 1812 was on. The war was ignited by the British blockade and seizure of U.S. ships and would be fought on U.S. soil. As in the Civil War and World Wars I and II, the incumbent president was reelected in the midst of a war. **James Madison** was returned for a second term, beating Federalist candidate, former U.S. Senator DeWitt Clinton. There was still no significant popular voting, and Madison won in the Electoral College, 128 votes to 89 over Clinton.

1816 . . .

The Democrat-Republicans were still the dominant party in the country while their opposition, the Federalists, became weaker and weaker. The Federalists didn't formally nominate a candidate for president but supported Rufus King of New York. King ran against Democrat-Republican **James Monroe**. Monroe won easily, 183 to 34 in the electoral votes.

1820 . . .

James Monroe turned out to be one of the most popular presidents in history. His first term in office was called the "era of good feeling." Incredibly, no one ran against him for a second term, and he got every electoral vote but one. The elector who voted against Monroe wasn't opposed to him, but felt no one except George Washington should be elected unanimously. That elector cast one lonely ballot for John Quincy Adams.

1824 . . .

Another bizarre election. James Monroe, following Washington and Jefferson's precedent, declined to run for a third term. This contest was between Andrew Jackson and John Quincy Adams, each representing different factions of the Democratic-Republican Party. Even though Jackson got the most electoral votes, no one received the necessary majority. As in 1800, the election was thrown into the House of Representatives. Jackson had beaten **John Quincy Adams** in the electoral voting, 99 to 84, but the House chose Adams as president when supporters of other candidates threw their votes to Adams.

1828 . . .

For the first time, popular votes became a real factor in presidential elections. **Andrew Jackson**, whose supporters thought he had been robbed in the 1824 election, won by more than 100,000 popular votes against incumbent John Quincy Adams. Like his father, Adams was denied a second term.

1832 . . .

Andrew Jackson scored another victory of more than 100,000 popular votes, this time against Senator Henry Clay. The old Federalist Party was out of business and the Democrat-Republicans had split into various branches. Jackson represented the Democratic wing, while Clay's branch was called National Republican. That was not the same as today's Republican Party, which would be formed later. The split in the Democrat-Republican party for this election was based mainly on tariffs. Clay favored high tariffs. Jackson did not.

1836 . . .

Andrew Jackson was a generally popular president who possibly could have been elected to a third term had he chosen to run. His party, the Democrats, picked **Martin Van Buren,** who beat William Henry Harrison by more than 200,000 votes. Harrison was the first presidential candidate of the Whig Party, which tended to be more conservative than Van Buren's Democratic Party.

1840 . . .

This time the Whigs put their first man in the White House when **William Henry Harrison** beat Martin Van Buren in a rematch of their 1836 election. It also broke the forty-year hold the Democrat-Republicans enjoyed in presidential elections. Van Buren's chances for a second term were damaged by the Financial Panic (the name then for a depression) that hit the nation in 1837.

1844 . . .

William Henry Harrison lasted only thirty-two days in office after winning the 1840 election. When he died of pneumonia, he was succeeded by Vice President John Tyler, who was derisively nicknamed "His Accidency." Tyler was not considered for his party's nomination for another term. The nomination by the Whigs went to Henry Clay, who had lost the 1832 election. Clay, a heavy favorite to win this time, was upset by Democrat **James Polk**, who was not well known nationally, but beat the over-confident Clay in a close race.

1848 . . .

James Polk claimed he disliked being president and announced early in his term that he would not run again. The Democrats turned to Senator Lewis Cass, but he was no match for war hero **Zachary Taylor**. Taylor brought the Whigs back to the presidency, but he died less than two years into his term. VP Millard Fillmore took over, and as it turned out, he was the last Whig to occupy the White House. Every president since then has been either a Democrat or Republican.

1852 . . .

Incumbent Millard Fillmore was not popular enough to be nominated for another term. His Whig Party picked General Winfield Scott instead. But Scott was trounced by Democrat **Franklin Pierce** by an 86 to 14 percent margin in the Electoral College. Pierce then spent a gloomy four years in office, marked by the personal tragedy of the death of his son and the subsequent depression of his wife. He would not be nominated for a second term.

1856 . . .

With the Civil War looming, the new Republican Party (the one still in existence today) came into being. The Republicans nominated Senator John Fremont as their first presidential candidate. But Fremont was beaten by the Democrat, **James Buchanan**, whom the nation hoped could solve the widening gap between the North and South.

1860 . . .

Many people thought that incumbent president James Buchanan had not done enough to stave off the growing rift between North and South, which would eventually lead to the Civil War. His Democratic party split into Northern and Southern divisions with the Northerners choosing Senator Stephen Douglas of Illinois to run for president. The Southerners picked Buchanan's VP, John Breckinridge of Kentucky. The Republicans nominated an Illinois man who had lost several previous U.S. Senate and state elections, but who had been an effective debater against Douglas. He was a man who would become one of the most famous presidents, **Abraham Lincoln**. Lincoln got 500,000 more votes than Douglas and a million more than Breckinridge. The war was just months away.

1864 . . .

There was little question that **Abraham Lincoln** would get a second term. His opponent in the election was General George McClellan, who lost to Lincoln by an Electoral College margin of 212 to 80. What was unknown was that Lincoln would be assassinated one month into his term. The new president was VP Andrew Johnson, who would struggle with reconstruction, and was not nominated to run in 1868.

1868 . . .

The Civil War was over and the Republicans happily nominated the Northern hero of the war, **General Ulysses Grant**. The Democrats turned to New York governor Horatio Seymour. But Seymour was no match for Grant. He lost the election by a 73 percent to 27 percent Electoral College margin.

1872 . . .

To combat **Ulysses Grant's** popularity, this time the Democrats selected the New York *Tribune* publisher Horace Greeley (of "Go West, young man" fame). Grant won big again—but Greeley wouldn't have been able to serve anyway. He died a few weeks after the election. This election was also notable for the third-party candidacy of the first woman to run for president, Victoria Woodhull. She ran on the Equal Rights Party platform.

1876 . . .

Another mixed-up election. Democrat Samuel Tilden got more popular votes than Republican **Rutherford Hayes**, but several key electoral votes were in dispute over the eligibility of some electors. The House of Representatives again had to decide who would be president. A special fifteen-man House committee voted along party lines to give the presidency to Hayes by the margin of eight to seven. Democrats agreed not to contest the vote in return for promises that federal reconstruction troops would be withdrawn from the South.

1880 . . .

Much like James Polk, incumbent Rutherford Hayes said he did not like being president and would not run for a second term. The Republicans nominated **James Garfield** to run against the Democrat, General Winfield Hancock. It was a close election with each candidate carrying nineteen of the then thirty-eight states, but Garfield had the edge in electoral votes and became the fourth Republican in a row to be elected president. His term would be short. He died from an assassin's bullet six months after taking office and was succeeded by VP Chester Arthur.

1884 . . .

The Democrats finally broke the string of Republican victories by running **Grover Cleveland** against former Secretary of State James Blaine. The incumbent president, Chester Arthur, was denied the nomination and faded into political oblivion. Republican Blaine came close, but lost in both popular and electoral voting.

1888 . . .

Trying for a second term, Grover Cleveland got almost 100,000 more popular votes than Republican **Benjamin Harrison**, but Harrison had a clear-cut win in electoral votes, 58 to 42 percent, and unseated Cleveland in yet another election where the popular-vote winner wound up being the loser. (This election, and others, fuels the argument of those who think the system should be changed.)

1892 . . .

For the only time in U.S. history, a former president was reelected to the White House. **Grover Cleveland** turned the tables on Benjamin Harrison, beating him decisively in both popular and electoral votes. Cleveland thus was both the twenty-second and twenty-fourth president.

1896 . . .

With the twelve-year Cleveland-Harrison saga over, the Democrats nominated a man who would become their three-time loser in presidential elections, the flamboyant orator William Jennings Bryan. The Republicans chose Ohio governor **William McKinley**, who parlayed his famous "Front Porch" stay-at-home campaign to a relatively easy win.

1900 . . .

William Jennings Bryan tried again to beat **William McKinley**, but lost even more convincingly this time around. However, McKinley's VP, Theodore Roosevelt, would soon become president. McKinley was assassinated six months into his second term as the nation marked its third presidential assassination in thirty-six years.

1904 . . .

Theodore Roosevelt had an easy time winning a full term in his own right, swamping a little-known New York judge, Alton Parker. Roosevelt, the youngest U.S. president, had great energy, advocating what he called "the strenuous life." He had gained national recognition as a famed Rough Rider in the Spanish-American War, was governor of New York, then vice president—and upon succeeding the assassinated William McKinley, swung into action with his "trust busting," conservation, and food safety initiatives. He led the nation into the new century, advocating that the U.S. should become a world power, "speaking softly but carrying a big stick."

1908 . . .

Although Theodore Roosevelt said he probably enjoyed being president more than any other man, he felt he should not run for a third term, and selected his secretary of war, **William Howard Taft**, to succeed him. Taft easily beat William Jennings Bryan, who lost for the third time as the Democratic presidential candidate.

1912 . . .

President William Howard Taft had a falling out with his benefactor, Theodore Roosevelt, and when Taft was nominated by the Republicans for a second term, Roosevelt decided to run against him as a third-party candidate on his Bull Moose or Progressive Party ticket. Roosevelt got more votes than Taft—but that Roosevelt-Taft battle split the Republicans, and gave the election to Democrat **Woodrow Wilson**, the former college professor and governor of New Jersey.

1916 . . .

World War I was on, although the U.S. had not yet entered it. **Woodrow Wilson** campaigned on the slogan "He kept us out of war," and beat the Republican, U.S. Supreme Court Justice Charles Evans Hughes by a slim margin. As it turned out, Wilson didn't keep the country out of war. The year after the election, the U.S. was in the war.

1920 . . .

A new era dawned in America. The war was over, and Republican **Warren Harding** ran on the platform of "returning to normalcy." Harding beat Ohio governor and publisher James Cox, but instead of normalcy, the nation entered the go-go, devil-may-care Roaring Twenties with rum-runners, flappers, the Jazz Age, and wild stock-market speculation. Harding served only two years before dying of natural causes, and was succeeded by VP Calvin Coolidge.

1924 . . .

Good times prevailed in America, and **Calvin Coolidge** had little trouble getting nominated for a full term after succeeding Warren Harding. The election was a breeze as Coolidge won by more than seven million votes against Constitutional lawyer, ambassador, and former congressman John Davis of West Virginia. "Keep Cool with Coolidge" was the Republican mantra, and the nation did.

1928 . . .

With prosperity still generally prevalent in the country, Calvin Coolidge could very possibly have been elected again. But in a surprise statement in 1927, Coolidge, never known for making speeches when he didn't have to, wrote a message on small slips of paper that he handed to reporters. The slips of paper said: "I do not choose to run for president in 1928." Republicans nominated Coolidge's secretary of commerce, **Herbert Hoover**. The Democrats nominated the first-ever major party candidate who was a Catholic, New York governor Al Smith. Hoover, a wealthy, popular philanthropist, defeated Smith by more than six million votes, as Americans wanted to keep the good times rolling.

1932 . . .

How times had changed. A little more than seven months after Herbert Hoover took office, the Roaring Twenties came to a screeching halt with the stock market crash. By the time the 1932 election was held, America was in the depths of the Great Depression. It was highly unlikely that Hoover could win a second term, but the Republicans nominated him anyway. Many in the party felt they'd lose no matter who they ran. The Democrats selected the charismatic, optimistic, inspiring **Franklin Roosevelt**, who would promise a "New Deal" for America. Roosevelt got 89 percent of the electoral vote to Hoover's 11 percent.

1936 . . .

In one of the biggest presidential landslides of all time, **Franklin Roosevelt** carried forty-six of the then forty-eight states. His opponent, Kansas governor Alf Landon, took only the then rock-ribbed Republican states of Maine and Vermont. An interesting footnote to the election was that a respected magazine, *The Literary Digest*, came out with a well-publicized poll before election day that predicted Landon would win. *The Literary Digest* went out of business soon after.

1940 . . .

No president had ever been elected three times, but with the nation slowly coming out of the traumatic Depression, and with the likelihood that America would soon be fighting in World War II, voters gave **Franklin Roosevelt** an unprecedented third term. His Republican opponent was a lawyer-businessman, Wendell Willkie, who seemed to come out of nowhere. He was not nationally prominent, but his anti-Roosevelt positions captured attention at the Republican convention and seemingly spontaneous chants of "We want Willkie" began to fill the hall. Although

Willkie didn't win the election, he did better against Roosevelt than Hoover and Landon, taking ten states.

1944 . . .

Three-term U.S. presidents were unheard of until **Franklin Roosevelt** came along—but four terms? It happened when Roosevelt got 81 percent of the electoral vote against against the 19 percent won by a former famous prosecuting district attorney and current New York governor, Thomas Dewey. With World War II still being fought, Americans apparently felt safer with the experienced Roosevelt at the helm. (No president ever again will serve as long as Roosevelt unless there's a new Constitutional amendment. Shortly after Roosevelt left office, an amendment was passed prohibiting any president from being elected more than twice.) Roosevelt's fourth term ended suddenly when he died of natural causes on April 12, 1945. He was succeeded by VP Harry Truman.

1948 . . .

Arguably the biggest presidential election surprise in history. **Harry Truman**, admittedly bewildered when he took over for Franklin Roosevelt, had begun to grow into the job, but almost every poll taken in the fall of 1948 indicated an easy win for Thomas Dewey. Truman's "Give 'em hell," whistle-stop campaign, and Dewey's probable overconfidence apparently turned the tide. Truman not only scored the presidential upset of the ages by simply winning, but he trounced Dewey in Electoral College voting, 303 to 189.

1952 . . .

Harry Truman endorsed the governor of Illinois, Adlai Stevenson, for the Democratic nomination, but there were several other strong candidates, including Estes Kefauver and Richard Russell. It took three ballots at the nominating convention, and Stevenson got the thankless job of running against the popular World War II hero **Dwight Eisenhower**. As expected, Eisenhower won easily.

1956 . . .

Americans were settling into post-war living, raising families with the baby boom. Conditions were generally good, Ike was popular, and there seemed to be no question he'd get a second term. **Dwight Eisenhower** was nominated by acclamation at the Republican convention. The Democrats again threw Adlai Stevenson into the battle for the presidency—but it was really no battle. Ike won by even a bigger landslide than the first time.

1960 . . .

This election marked the first time two presidential nominees debated face-to-face on live, national TV. The nation was riveted not only by this milestone, but by the opposing debaters—the young, photogenic **John Kennedy** and the incumbent, sometimes ill-at-ease vice president Richard Nixon. Kennedy seemed to score victory in the debates—but the election was surprisingly close. Kennedy got 49.7 percent of the popular vote to 49.5 for Nixon, the closest popular vote up to that time in history.

1964 . . .

When John Kennedy, in 1963, became the fourth president to be assassinated, VP **Lyndon Johnson** moved into the Oval Office, and then was unanimously nominated on the first ballot to run for president in his own right in 1964. A leading conservative, Senator Barry Goldwater of Arizona, delivered a memorable—and to some, controversial—quote, when he accepted the Republican nomination. Goldwater said, "Extremism in the defense of liberty is no vice. And moderation in the pursuit of justice is no virtue." The election was a rout. Johnson got more than fifteen million more votes than Goldwater, and carried forty-four of the fifty states.

1968 . . .

By the end of Lyndon Johnson's term, America was sharply divided over the Vietnam War. Increasing anti-war protests and a youth rebellion were tearing the nation apart. Johnson went on national TV in March of 1968 to announce he would not run for another term because of the split over the war. At the contentious Democratic convention, with street riots taking place outside, Johnson's VP, Hubert Humphrey, was nominated to run for president. The Republicans picked the man who had lost the 1960 presidential election and, in a bitter "farewell" after being beaten in the 1962 California governor's race, said, "You won't have **Richard Nixon** to kick around anymore." But in the 1968 presidential election, Nixon made a remarkable comeback, carrying thirty-two states to Humphrey's thirteen, with third-party candidate George Wallace taking five.

1972 . . .

In one of the biggest routs in presidential history, **Richard Nixon** crushed the hopes of the Democrats and their candidate, Senator George McGovern of South Dakota. Nixon won by almost eighteen million votes and carried every state except Massachusetts and the District of Columbia. But the clouds of the Watergate scandal were starting to engulf Nixon, and two years into his second term he resigned the presidency, concluding a tumultuous career of extreme highs and achievements combined with brutal lows and failures.

1976 . . .

Gerald Ford was in the White House by virtue of being selected vice president when Spiro Agnew resigned, and then becoming president when Richard Nixon resigned. Ford was nominated to run for his own term, facing a formerly nationally unknown peanut farmer and governor of Georgia, **Jimmy Carter**. Ford was hurt by his pardon of Richard Nixon and some verbal gaffes on the campaign trail, and Carter became the first president from the Deep South since before the Civil War. Carter won the relatively close election by a little more than one million votes and a fifty-seven-vote electoral margin.

1980 . . .

Jimmy Carter tried for a second term, but a weak economy and hostages being held in the U.S. embassy in Iran doomed his chances. Along came the "Great Communicator," **Ronald Reagan,** as the Republican candidate. Reagan won in a landslide, getting 489 electoral votes to Carter's forty-nine. The American hostages in Iran were released on inauguration day, just after Reagan had been sworn in. Carter never ran for elective office again, but performed humanitarian work and mediated international disputes.

1984 . . .

Ronald Reagan set a record by getting more popular votes than any other president up to this time, with a total of 54,281,858. His Democratic opponent, former vice president Walter Mondale, carried only one state—his home state of Minnesota. History was also made in this election with a groundbreaking first. A woman was on a major-party ticket for vice president, as New York congresswoman Geraldine Ferraro was chosen as Mondale's running mate.

1988 . . .

Ronald Reagan's two-term vice president, **George H. W. Bush**, won a fairly easy contest against the Democratic governor of Massachusetts, Michael Dukakis, by more than seven million votes. Bush would achieve one of the highest approval ratings in presidential history midway through his term after the Persian Gulf War. But his popularity quickly fell the next year when the economy slipped into a recession, and questions arose about whether he could be elected to a second term.

1992 . . .

Arkansas governor **Bill Clinton** came upon the national scene as an effective campaigner, surprisingly winning most of the presidential primaries. Despite some questions about his character, he secured the Democratic nomination to run against incumbent George Bush. Also in the race was third-party candidate Ross Perot, who turned out to be a factor, getting more than nineteen million votes in the election. Bush received thirty-nine million, but Clinton got more than forty-four million, and was on his way to the White House.

1996 . . .

This time, the Republicans picked longtime senator Bob Dole to run against **Bill Clinton**. But it was largely no contest. Ross Perot ran again as a third-party candidate. However, Perot's vote total slipped from more than nineteen million in 1992 to just more than eight million in 1996. Clinton got three million more votes than he had four years earlier, and Dole had a million fewer than Bush in the previous election. Clinton became the first Democratic president elected to two terms since Franklin Roosevelt, sixty years earlier.

2000 . . .

Other presidential elections had controversial vote

counts—but this one moved from polling places, to state courts, and finally, to the U.S. Supreme Court before the nation knew who would be their next president. Bill Clinton's VP, Al Gore, got about 540,000 more popular votes nationally than **George W. Bush**, but the issue was the twenty-five electoral votes for Florida. Whoever won that state would win the election. Bush had a small lead in the Florida votes, but the Democrats challenged the count. A month after the election, on December 8, after many hearings in lower courts, the Florida Supreme Court ordered a partial recount. But on December 12, the U.S. Supreme Court reversed that decision, effectively giving Bush the twenty-five electoral votes he needed for victory. The next day, Gore conceded the election to Bush.